George Washington Carver

George Washington Carver

by
Fern Neal Stocker

A Guessing Book

MOODY PRESS
CHICAGO

Library of Congress Cataloging in Publication Data

Stocker, Fern Neal, 1917-
    George Washington Carver / by Fern Neal Stocker ; [illustrations
are by Virginia Hughins].
        p.   cm. — (A Guessing book)
    Summary: A biography of the famous scientist emphasizing his
partnership with God in making his discoveries. Multiple choice
questions are interspersed throughout the text to entertain the
reader.
    ISBN 0-8024-4759-7
    1. Carver, George Washington, 1864?-1943—Juvenile literature.
2. Agriculturists—United States—Biography—Juvenile literature.
[1. Carver, George Washington, 1864?-1943.   2. Agriculturists.
3. Afro-Americans—Biography.   4. Literary recreations.]
I. Hughins, Virginia, ill.   II. Title.   III. Series: Stocker, Fern
Neal, 1917-   Guessing book.
S417.C3S76   1987
630'.92'4—dc19
[B]
[92]

ISBN: 0-8024-4759-7

2 3 4 5 6 7 Printing/LC/Year 92 91 90 89

Printed in the United States of America

To my son, Paul

Contents

To You, the Reader:

A Guessing Book is the story of a famous person. As you read along in this Guessing Book, you'll come to questions you can answer by yourself.

One, two, or three guesses are given, and you can choose one, two, or three answers. Sometimes all are correct, sometimes none. (You'll find the answer as you keep reading.) Pretty soon you'll know the person in the story so well you can get the answer right every time.

It may be fun to keep track of how many guesses you get right. But if you miss one, don't worry—this isn't a test.

Read this Guessing Book and learn about George Washington Carver, a man who followed God's plan for his life.

1

Thanksgiving

George wished he could be as happy as Aunt Susan and Uncle Moses. But he couldn't. Uncle Richard's family coming for Thanksgiving only meant

GUESS

1. trouble for George.
2. two against one.
3. more food for George.

"This means trouble," George worried. "When Dick and Jim get together, I always get the short end of everything." He watched his older brother as he listened to Aunt Susan read the letter.

"Yippie day! What fun!" Jim burst out, as Aunt Susan finished reading.

Uncle Moses smiled. "Yes, we've all worked hard this year and deserve a holiday."

"That we do!" Aunt Susan nodded, perhaps remembering her pantry loaded with

GUESS

1. potatoes and watermelons.
2. jams and jellies.
3. fruits and vegetables.

"My pantry is full of jars of fruit, vegetables, and jellies. There are potatoes and melons in the root cellar," Aunt Susan declared. "We have plenty for all, even if they do have seven children."

When Aunt Susan jumped up, folded the letter, and walked toward the kitchen, George followed. He knew Jim would join Uncle Moses beside the fireplace in their log cabin.

"Aunt Sue," George began,

GUESS	1. "I'll run away." 2. "I'll help you in the kitchen." 3. "I won't play."

George said, "I'll help you in the kitchen."

Aunt Susan said, "No, you'll play with the others."

George scowled. Aunt Susan took her arms out of the dishwater and held his black face between her white hands. "I know they tease you, and you can't help that! Is that what's bothering you?"

"They tell me lies! Then they laugh when I believe them."

"Well, you just laugh back. You can't help what *they* do, but you can help what *you* do. Don't let *them* hurt you. They tease because it bothers you."

George answered,

GUESS	1. "I can't laugh." 2. "I hate them." 3. "I'll try to laugh."

George answered, "I'll try, but . . ."

Thanksgiving dawned cold and clear. Jim, George, and Uncle Moses got up at 4:00 A.M. As usual, they milked the cows and fed the animals. The year was 1874. On their farm at the foot of the Ozarks in Diamond Grove, Missouri, the family felt thankful, for they had everything they needed. They had

1. sheep to shear.

12

GUESS 2. whale blubber to cut.
3. wool and flax to spin.

They had sheep to shear, flax to spin, deerskins to tan, shoes to make, horses to tend, and wood to split. "The only things we buy are coffee and sugar—and mighty little of that," Uncle Moses boomed in his deep German voice.

George wished he had a deep voice like that.

By ten o'clock the cabin swarmed with little white children. "Outside! Outside all of you!" Aunt Susan yelled over the din. "How can your mother and I get the dinner on the table with you running everywhere?"

The little children grabbed jackets or coats and fled ahead of Aunt Susan. They tumbled over each other to get to the barn.

Dick called to them, "Anyone who has fifteen cents can play with us big boys!"

GUESS 1. Two children stopped.
2. Only Larry stopped.
3. Four hesitated.

Only eight-year-old Larry halted in the pell mell rush. He came back to where the big boys, Dick, Jim, and George, stood. "What you doing?" he asked.

Dick held up a dime and a nickel. "I'll bet fifteen cents that you can put on your shoes and tie them anyway you want—hard as you can—and run around the house three times." He paused and patted Jim. "Jim, here, will be the inspector. I bet your shoes will be on-tied after the run. If they are on-tied, I win your fifteen cents. Jim holds the money, so it's fair."

George and Larry looked at each other. George realized Dick knew that Larry had fifteen cents in his pocket, and Jim knew George had fifteen pennies in a jar in the kitchen cupboard. George thought about the money. *I saved for so long,* he thought. George finally said,

1. "I'll bet."

| GUESS |

2. "I won't bet."
3. "I don't want to bet."

"I don't want to bet," he said.

"Why not?" Dick teased. "You can't tie your shoes yet? You're afraid your knots won't hold? A black slave child can't even tie a good knot?"

"A black boy can tie knots good as a white boy any day!" George exploded. He knew his knots would hold, so why not bet? Quickly he slipped into the kitchen and brought back the jar with his fifteen precious pennies. "Here, hold it, Jim!" he exclaimed, as he fell to his knees and retied one shoe after the other. "There, I'm ready," he said.

Larry was ready, too, having given Jim his fifteen cents while George was in the kitchen.

"Ready, set, go!" Dick called the words slowly, one at a time. As Larry and George ran around the house, they kept rather close together.

"One," Dick called as they passed. "Two," as they rounded the house again, and, "Three," as the younger boys puffed up before them for the third time.

Jim inspected the shoes. He pointed at Larry's shoes. "Still tied tight," he pronounced. Then he examined George's. "As firm as when he started," Jim stated.

The decision was that

| GUESS |

1. George won.
2. Larry won.
3. Dick won.

"Then we won!" George cried.

"Not so fast!" Dick held up his hand. "I said I'd win if *your shoes was on and tied!* On-tied, remember? Give me the money, Jim." Dick and Jim laughed in the younger boys' faces. Larry ran to the house to tell his mother, but George

1. remembered Aunt Susan's words.

14

"Ready, set, go!"

| GUESS |

2. laughed.
3. started a fight.

George remembered Aunt Susan's words. He laughed so hard that he fell on the ground and rolled. He tried to make his laughter sound funny, and he succeeded well enough to fool Dick and Jim.

"You're a good sport!" Dick said. "I thought you'd be mad."

"Let's play mumble peg," George suggested, bringing out a knife with a black handle and two blades. The three boys made a triangle and began playing.

"That's George's dream knife," Jim said.

"What you mean?"

"He dreamed about the knife. In his dream he saw a watermelon in a patch, and a knife stuck in it."

"That's a lie!" Dick challenged. "The knife is real."

"Yes," George said. "I recognized the watermelon patch in the dream and went there the next day. I found

| GUESS |

1. no knife."
2. a rusty knife."
3. the black handled knife."

"Right there was the knife stuck in the watermelon like I dreamed it," George explained.

"You're making up a story!"

"No, it's true," Jim added. "I went with him."

After they had played for an hour, the smells from the kitchen tickled their noses.

"Come to dinner," Aunt Susan finally called.

"I'm tired of George winning every game, anyway," Dick grumbled.

Even the thirty cents in his pocket doesn't comfort him, George thought. *I really won, even if it cost me fifteen cents.*

The children viewed the table, and their eyes widened when they saw turkey and ham with corn, potatoes, and fresh slaw; great slices of dark bread with fresh churned butter and jam. On a nearby table the pumpkin pies and chocolate cake vied with nuts and fruits for attention. George never forgot the sight, especially on the many days when he had nothing to eat.

After dinner the small ones settled down for naps. Emma said, "Dick, read to the older children while the adults sit down to a peaceful dinner."

George was jealous because

GUESS
1. Dick and Jim were larger.
2. Jim worked in the fields.
3. Dick could read.

George was not jealous of their size or work; he was jealous because Dick could read. Dick's white skin allowed him to go to the Locust Grove School only a mile away.

As George listened to Dick read, he remembered the days he sat on the doorstep of the school. He didn't do that anymore since

GUESS
1. the teacher welcomed him.
2. the little children invited him.
3. older children told him to leave.

The older children had told him, "We don't allow colored young 'uns in here."

After that he hid himself in the woods with his friends—the trees, the flowers, and the rocks. They didn't mind his color. He studied the blue spelling book Aunt Susan gave him, and he memorized all the words. "But that's not reading!" he muttered to himself, listening to his cousin Dick. "My *cousin*, that's what Uncle Moses says, but he knows he's not *really* my cousin. My mother and father were slaves. Uncle Moses says Jim and I are free, and he pretends we are sons, but I don't feel free."

After playing with Larry until sundown, George was glad to hear Uncle Richard call out,

GUESS
1. "Let's beat the sun home."
2. "We'll have to leave soon."
3. "Let's sing before we go."

17

Uncle Richard called everyone together to sing before they went home.

Obediently George got the fiddle he had made out of a cornstalk and the bow made with horsetail hairs.

Uncle Richard listened to the children singing with the four adults. When they finished, he beamed. "Cornstalk fiddle and ransum bow makes best old music you ever did know." His family laughed as they tumbled into the wagon and started toward home.

As soon as everyone was gone, George and Aunt Susan cleaned up. In the kitchen George announced, "Aunt Susan, I want to go to school. I want to learn."

2

Plant Doctor

Georize was often sick. From his bed he would watch Aunt
Susan brew roots and herbs to make a healing tea. He felt
her loving hands rub his hurting legs with a salve made from bark
juice and tallow.

"I feel better now," he said and then helped weave cloth, tan
deer skin, or make shoes.

Uncle Moses, however, thought men could make better shoes.
After making himself a new pair from tanned deer leather, he

GUESS	1. limped.
	2. swore.
	3. soaked his blisters.

Uncle Moses did all three things and complained so loudly that
George took the new shoes apart one night as they sat by the fire.

Carefully he shaped the shoes to Uncle Moses' feet and sewed
them together again. Then he re-wove the old man's socks. "Try
them now, Uncle Moses," he said.

"I'd never believe the difference," Uncle Moses admitted. "A
shoemaker I'm not!"

Neither could he answer George's questions. "Where does the

sun go behind the hill?" or, "Why are the roses by the door yellow, and those under the window red?"

On Sundays the Carvers did not attend church, but neither did they do unnecessary work. George spent his time in the woods. He poked beneath the tree bark and watched insects crawl. He found that some flowers

GUESS	1. wanted sun.
	2. wanted storms.
	3. wanted shade.

He said, "Different flowers want different things. Some want sun and some shade, some clay and some sand, some water and some dryness." He wondered what happened to the fluff from the milkweed pods. "Ferns and flowers are my friends," he whispered as he played and talked to them.

For Sunday lunch he ate corn dodgers. Corn dodgers are sandwiches made of

GUESS	1. peanut butter.
	2. fat meat and cornbread.
	3. ham and cheese.

Corn dodgers are sandwiches made of fat salt pork and cornbread.

One day Jim watched George in the woods. He saw the sun filtering through the trees making patches of light and shade. He watched George touch the flowers, talk to them, and give them water. After a while, Jim said, "What you doing to them flowers?"

George answered,

GUESS	1. "How dare you watch me?"
	2. "I'm loving them."
	3. "Throwing dirt at them."

"I'm loving them," George answered.

Together they walked back to the cabin. George held a handful of dirt. As they walked, he let it sift through his fingers. "There's life in dirt, Jim."

"No, there's not. You're crazy, George!"

When they reached the cabin, they saw that Aunt Susan had company. Together she and a well-dressed woman were looking at the roses under the cabin window.

"Who's she?" George asked.

"That's the lady from the Grant place. You know, the one with the big house and the fire-red hair."

When they approached, Aunt Susan motioned the boys closer. "This is Mrs. Fred Baynham." Motioning to the boys, she said, "These are Carvers, George and Jim."

The boys nodded, and Mrs. Baynham smiled as she said, "How do you do?" Then she put out her hand to George and said, "I understand you are a plant doctor, and I see your beautiful roses here. Mine never looked like this. My roses must be sick. Could you come over and look at them one day?" She leaned down to look directly into George's eyes.

George nodded. He

GUESS	1. couldn't say anything.
	2. was angry.
	3. was shy.

George was shy. He never knew if white folks would be kind or cruel. He thought, *Aunt Susan called me a plant doctor.* That made him feel good all over.

Next day he walked to the old Grant place. Seeing no one about, he sought out the roses in the yard. "You poor things." He sighed. "You want sun, and they put you in the shade. You want some water, but they drown you." In a few minutes he had dug holes on a hillside and moved the roses into the sun. "Now, I'll give you a drink, and every time it rains you'll get water but not enough to keep your feet wet. Hope you are happy here."

Still seeing no one, he walked to the house, wiped his feet as Aunt Susan had taught him, and lifted the knocker. The door was open, and George peeked inside. On the wall he saw a painting of a bowl of flowers. George

21

GUESS

1. stepped inside.
2. ran away.
3. stood still.

The picture drew him inside, and George stepped closer to examine the lovely colors.

"Do you like it?" Mrs. Baynham slipped up beside the enchanted boy.

"Oh, yes, ma'am. How did they make it?"

"It's a painting. I have more in the living room. Won't you come in?"

George followed. He saw pictures of forests, flowers, landscapes, and even paintings of men and women.

"Oh, they are so pretty!" he exclaimed.

Finally the hostess showed him her canvas and paints. "See, you dip the brush and paint so," she said, demonstrating.

"Oh, ma'am, how do you learn?" George gasped.

"Well, I attended an art school."

"You learn that in school, too?" George suddenly realized he was standing in a grand living room on a real carpet. He

GUESS

1. felt the rug.
2. ran away.
3. blushed.

George fled toward the door.

The woman caught him before he escaped, however, and pressed a nickel into his hand. "That's for doctoring my roses," she said.

"Oh, I couldn't take it," George objected. "You let me see the pictures. That's enough." He escaped, leaving the nickel on a nearby table.

"What?" Jim scolded, as soon as George told the story at home. "You crazy? You didn't take a whole nickel?"

Aunt Susan smiled. "George got more than a nickel. He got eyes aglow."

George squeezed pokeberries and boiled barks to make colors. Then he painted

22

<table>
<tr><td>GUESS</td><td>1. with a horsehair brush.
2. on flat rocks.
3. on old cans and buckets.</td></tr>
</table>

He painted outside on rocks with his horsehair brush.

On the cover of his blue spelling book, George studied a picture of a man climbing a high cliff. A large building was on top. Aunt Susan called it the temple of learning. George painted the picture on an enormous rock down by the creek.

"That's me," he said, pointing to the climbing man. "I've got to find the temple of learning soon."

Occasionally he and Jim were allowed to walk to the town of Neosho, eight miles away.

One Saturday they saw the fancy wagon of the medicine man. George listened to the man's speech but thought, *Aunt Sue can make better medicine from herbs and plants.*

They loitered on the wooden sidewalks, gazing into the general store, the hat shop, and the harness shop. They listened to the banjo pickers. Several times they looked at the big courthouse on the square. The building rose two stories high.

Finally they walked to the edge of town, and there George saw a building. The sign said "Lincoln School for Colored Children." George couldn't read the sign, so he

<table>
<tr><td>GUESS</td><td>1. walked away, never knowing.
2. asked Jim to read it.
3. figured it out.</td></tr>
</table>

George looked at the building. It was shaped like the Locust Grove School, but *black* children played on the steps and in the yard.

"What you doing?" George asked.

"Playing."

"What's this you're playing on?"

"The steps of the school, dummy!"

"A school for whites?" George was cautious.

"No, a school for colored. See, it says, 'Lincoln School for Colored Children.' Can't you read?"

"No, but I will soon!" George told them.

After he returned to the farm, he announced, "Uncle Moses, I want to go to school. There's a school for coloreds in Neosho, and I'm going!"

"But how? Where will you stay?"

"Honey, you are only ten years old and small for that," Aunt Susan objected. "How will you live? Eat?"

"I don't know, but I'll find a way. I declare I will."

"I can't stop you, George. You're free." Uncle Moses looked over George's head at Aunt Sue. "I won't try to stop you, but it beats me how you can do it."

Aunt Susan threw her arms around George. "I'll get your clothes ready. But always remember you are welcome here at home. A filled head in no wise satisfies an empty stomach."

3

Neosho

George walked the eight miles to Neosho. "Aunt Susan and Uncle Moses do love me." He swallowed his sobs as he held tight to his bundle of clean clothes and corn dodgers. "But I have to learn to read, to paint, to do figures. I just have to."

Jim had promised to

GUESS	1. stay for the harvest.
	2. go with George.
	3. stay in Diamond Grove.

Jim had promised to follow George after the harvest, but George didn't expect him. *Jim doesn't care about learning like I do,* he thought.

George saw the sun sinking behind the Ozark mountains when he reached Neosho. He found his way through the quiet streets. He finally located the schoolhouse, deserted at this time of night. There, he sat on the steps and ate the last of his corn dodgers.

"This is the poor part of town, it's easy to see," George mused. He saw

1. gold mansions.

GUESS

2. beautiful shiny windows.

3. sagging fences.

The sagging fences and broken windows stuffed with rags told him, "These people are poor."

"But on this side of the street, there's one neat house, painted even, with a wood lot, a stout barn, and a pasture," he said to himself. In the backyard, George could see battered wash tubs and a long clothesline.

Only a fence separated the farm from the school. "I'll sleep in the barn tonight and come back for school tomorrow," he decided.

George entered the barn and climbed to the hayloft. He had no trouble sleeping through the night. If he was cold, he didn't know it, for he was too tired to care.

George awoke before daybreak and lay in the hay for a few minutes. "Brrr, I'm cold and stiff," he muttered. "Better move around." He climbed down the loft ladder and took a brisk run up the street and back. "Feel warmer," he muttered, sitting on the woodpile beside the barn.

A stout black woman burst from the back door of the neat house. She stopped suddenly, put her hands on her hips, and stared at George. She said,

GUESS

1. "What you doing here, boy?"

2. "Get off my property."

3. "Bring in some wood."

The woman smiled. "Bring in some sticks, and we'll have breakfast. You look like you need a full belly."

George quickly gathered the wood and followed her into the warm kitchen. Soon bacon and eggs fried on the wood stove. George smelled the tangy bacon and heard the sizzle as he set the table.

"What's your name?" the black woman asked.

"I'm Carver's George."

"You mean George Carver, don't you? You're not a slave to be owned. Never call yourself that again. You hear? You're free now, *George Carver!*"

"I know I'm free. Uncle Moses always said I was free."

"Then act it!" The woman grinned, giving George a pat on his back. "My name's Watkins. Call me Aunt Mariah, and this here is Uncle Andy. He's the farmer, and I'm the town washerwoman."

Uncle Andy extended his hand. "George Carver. Hm, has a nice sound to it."

Soon they were seated around the table, and Aunt Mariah asked more questions.

"Where you come from?"

"From Diamond Grove—Carver's farm."

"Why you here?"

"I want to learn. To go to the Lincoln School. I learned all the words in the blue spelling book, but I still can't read."

Aunt Mariah studied George's face, thin and eager, but not plump like most boys his age.

"Where you staying?" Uncle Andy interposed.

George said,

| GUESS |

1. "In the schoolhouse."
2. "Under the house."
3. "In the barn."

"Well, last night I slept in the hayloft of yonder barn," George admitted. "I'm starting school today."

"Today you ain't," Aunt Mariah stated. "It's Saturday, and there's no school Saturday and Sunday."

"Oh." Disappointment showed on George's face.

When the meal was over, George waved Aunt Mariah aside, as she picked up the plates. "Here comes the best dishwasher you ever did see. Let me do it."

Aunt Mariah stepped aside but kept a sharp eye on George's actions.

"I see you are a good dishwasher. Who taught you?"

"Aunt Susan. She taught me to make candles and soap, to wash clothes, to iron, cook, weave, and even to sew."

"You are joshing me." Aunt Mariah laughed.

"Oh, no. I can cook," George objected. "Since there's no school, I'll cook dinner for you."

"You serious?" Aunt Mariah questioned sharply. "Well, I ad-

27

mit you do a good job with the dishes."

That evening George made dinner, and Uncle Andy pronounced it

| GUESS | 1. good.
2. just dandy.
3. terrible. |

"Just dandy!" Uncle Andy grinned. "Tell me about your parents," he asked kindly.

"Well, Mother was the Carver's only slave. Sally, they called her. She married with a slave from the Grant place, but he was sold off before I was born."

"That's what makes me so mad!" Aunt Mariah exploded, then shut her mouth firmly to keep from saying more. "What happened to your mother?"

"She

| GUESS | 1. died."
2. was stolen."
3. became queen." |

"During the war the raiders came and stole Mother and me. I was just a baby. They stole us away from the Carvers. I guess they didn't see my brother, Jim. Anyway, Uncle Moses sent a man after us. Promised him forty acres to bring us back." George paused.

"Did he bring you back?"

"Yes, he found me, but the raiders had either killed Mother or taken her someplace else. So Uncle Moses traded the man a horse to get me back."

"And they raised you and your brother?"

"Yes, they was always good to us. Jim worked in the fields with Uncle Moses, and I helped Aunt Sue do everything."

"But now you want to leave." Aunt Mariah smiled. "It's time, boy. It's time you lived with your own kind of folks. Get ready for your bath. We go to church on Sundays."

Uncle Andy looked up questioningly. Aunt Mariah said,

GUESS	1. "George is dirty." 2. "George is going to church." 3. "George is staying."

"George is staying with us a spell," Aunt Mariah said firmly.
"Oh, how lucky I am!" George squealed in his high voice.
"Luck has nothing to do with it," Aunt Mariah said. "Don't you see? The Lord brought you to us."
George sat in the African Methodist Church the next day and did as he was told. He couldn't help thinking,

GUESS	1. "I hate church." 2. "I wish I were in the woods." 3. "I like church."

George loved the music, but the thought, *I wish I were in the woods now, but anyways tomorrow is a school day.*

Aunt Mariah inspected George on Monday morning. "Remember your name, boy. Learn quick. Our people is hungry to know things."

George took the little money Uncle Moses had given him and climbed the fence.

Children swarmed everywhere. "Must be a million," he muttered.

The teacher, Steven Frost, introduced himself and sold George a book, slate, and slate pencil before he rang the bell. George filed in with other pupils of all ages.

The school was only 14 by 16 feet. George squeezed in on a long high bench made of rough boards. He thought, *I can hardly move.* Soon he realized, *It is up to me to do the learning, for the teacher is too busy keeping order.*

Mostly George learned from the other children. He was honored the first week, because he

GUESS	1. was a football hero. 2. won the first spell-down. 3. could give recitations.

On George's first Friday afternoon, Mr. Frost announced a spelling bee. To George's surprise, the words came from his old blue spelling book. Since he knew them all, he won the spell-down.

"How can you spell the words and still not read?" the other children marveled.

"It won't be long," George answered. "I've been listening to all the grades. I'm about to get the hang of it."

George learned

GUESS	1. slowly.
	2. quickly.
	3. steadily.

George's life grew into a steady routine—milking and feeding animals, breakfast, school, over the fence to the Watkins's at noon, rubbing clothes on the scrub board for an hour, gulping corn pone and sausage, and back over the fence for school in the afternoon.

After school George chopped and brought in the wood and milked the cows before Aunt Mariah served a hot meal. Then, they both attacked the books, for Aunt Mariah had determined to learn to read herself.

"I'm going to school right alongside of you, George," Aunt Mariah declared, as she stumbled over the words in the reader. "We are steady learners. Someday we'll know as much as the teacher."

Then what? George wondered. *I'm afraid that's not enough for me.*

4

Moving On

Georgia lived with the Watkins for

GUESS

1. three years.
2. two years.
3. five years.

George stayed with Aunt Mariah and Uncle Andy for three years. Then he explained to Aunt Mariah as they ate supper one evening, "Steven Frost is so busy teaching his younger children to read, write, and do simple arithmetic, he has no time for us. Also, there are no

GUESS

1. books."
2. libraries."
3. recess periods."

"Mr. Frost sends us older children outside for long recess periods. He only has two sets of books of his own, *Shakespeare's Works* and the Bible. 'Memorize these,' he tells us." George paused and looked into Aunt Mariah's brown eyes. "Most of the older children

GUESS

1. memorize whole books."
2. quit school."
3. tell their parents."

"Most older children convince their parents they have *learned it all* and quit school."

"Are you quitting?" Aunt Mariah asked.

"I've memorized long passages from the Bible, but I'll never learn it all."

Jim finally joined George, but he didn't like school. "I don't want to learn with the first graders," Jim objected. "I don't like the teacher, either."

So George was not surprised when Jim

GUESS

1. ran away.
2. took a job.
3. sat with the babies.

Jim said, "I found a man who will teach me plastering. I'm quitting school and taking the job in Neosha."

"I'm still staying on," George said. "I found another book belonging to my teacher. It's *The Dime Ludicrous Speaker,* and I've memorized several comic recitations."

"What are they?" Jim asked.

"A lecture on women's rights, which makes the pupils laugh. One titled 'Where the Hen Scratches, There She Expects to Find the Bug,' and Mark Twain's, 'Good Little Boy.' Mr. Frost has me recite on Friday afternoons. He says, 'George, you are very laughable.' "

But George didn't want to be laughable. He wanted

GUESS

1. to have his questions answered.
2. to paint.
3. to be a boxer.

"Three years," he told Aunt Mariah, "and I still don't know the answers. Where does the sun go? Why are flowers different colors? Why do frogs croak?"

Aunt Mariah shook her head sadly. "Mr. Frost doesn't know either. But everything has a purpose. God has a plan, and you must find it."

"I'm like a plant that needs to be moved in order to grow," George decided.

"Your pot is too small, I'm afraid." Aunt Mariah looked sternly into his eyes for a long moment. Then she added, "But always remember one thing, George. *When you do learn something, give it back to your own people.*" She paused. "Do you know the Smith family is moving to Fort Scott in the free state of Kansas?"

"No, would they take me?"

The Smith family

GUESS	1. refused to take George.
	2. agreed to take George.
	3. was too crowded.

The Smith family agreed.

George and Jim walked around town on one of their last days together. They also

GUESS	1. had a fight.
	2. had their pictures made.
	3. rode in an airplane.

They walked to Diamond Grove to say good-bye to the Carvers and gave them the picture they had taken together.

"I'll keep it always." Aunt Susan cried. "You know when you left, I always expected you back home any day!" She hugged the boys fiercely.

Just before he left, George went to see Steven Frost for a last farewell. "You've done well," the teacher said. "Here is a Certificate of Merit. When you present it at another school, they will recognize you as a serious scholar."

Mr. Frost hugged George for the first time. "Good luck, little friend. I wish I could have helped you more, but no teacher can handle seventy-five pupils."

The wagons creaked and pots and pans jangled the whole long trip to Fort Scott. Everyone who could walked to spare the mules. Fortunately it was downhill most of the way to level country. When George looked up into the sky, he felt

| GUESS |

1. sickness.
2. weariness.
3. prayers.

George felt Aunt Mariah's prayers, especially in the dark as he slept on the ground. "Someone is watching over me," he told himself. "I hope this is the right thing to do."

Once in Fort Scott, George was on his own. "Don't worry about me," he told the Smiths. "I'll get a job right away."

Bravely he walked the streets, stopping now and then at a friendly looking house. Everywhere he asked for work, he was told, "No houseboy is needed." They also directed him to always go to the back door.

Finally he came to a street with large homes and fine lawns. When he saw toys in a yard, around to the back door he went. A pretty young white woman answered his knock.

"Who are you?" she asked.

"I'm a houseboy," George said, forcing a smile. "I can cook, clean, do dishes, wash, and iron."

The young woman, Mrs. Payne, looked doubtful. "Did you say cook?" she asked.

"Yes, ma'am! I've had lots of practice." George thought he was telling the truth, because he knew every way to cook corn and pork.

"Hm." The woman hesitated. "I guess we could try you out."

They entered a kitchen such as George had never seen. It was shiny and white. New gadgets caught his eye. He saw a pump beside the sink, so that there was no need to go outside for water. The stove even had a tank on the side to keep the water warm.

"Now, for dinner we are having . . ." The woman named the dishes.

George

34

Who will watch over George now?

| GUESS | 1. knew how to cook everything.
| | 2. had never heard of such food.
| | 3. felt like crying.

George thought, *I've never even heard of such dishes.* He felt frantic.

"My husband is very fussy about his food. It has to be done just as he likes it," the woman explained.

George said,

| GUESS | 1. "I'm sorry, I can't do it."
| | 2. "You need someone else."
| | 3. "You will have to cook it yourself."

George didn't say anything. He looked at the pleasant lady and suggested, "Ma'am, since your husband wants his food a certain way, could you show me once? Then I can always do it as you do."

"That's a good idea," Mrs. Payne agreed. "Here, I do it this way." She proceeded to show George where the utensils were and how much of each item she used.

George memorized each step. He had always made corn muffins, but Mrs. Payne made biscuits with white wheat flour. The boy watched her as she kneaded the dough, rolled it out, and cut it with a biscuit cutter. While she was gone for several minutes tending her children, George washed all the dirty pots and pans.

"Good for you!" Mrs. Payne approved. "I always have such a mess in the kitchen, I hate to come back here after dinner."

The real test came with later dinners, which George cooked by himself. Mr. Payne was

| GUESS | 1. pleased.
| | 2. enthusiastic.
| | 3. resentful.

Mr. Payne soon liked George's cooking better than his wife's.

George became so good at making bread and biscuits that Mrs. Payne entered them in a Fort Scott fair.

"George, you've won in three categories—yeast bread, salt-rising bread, and buttermilk biscuits!" Mrs. Payne beamed. "Everyone was so surprised."

For some time George worked such long hours that he didn't attend school. Thus he saved some money. Sundays he spent in the woods. He painted whenever and however he could.

Finally he told Mrs. Payne he wanted

GUESS	1. to play the piano.
	2. to paint.
	3. to go to school.

"Why didn't you tell me sooner?" Mrs. Payne scolded. "We can arrange your work so you can go to school. The evening meal is most important anyway."

So George started school again—this time in a big brick building on the square.

"Oh, Mrs. Payne," he said. "I like my classes in arithmetic and geography."

"How about your class in nature study?" Mrs. Payne inquired.

"Oh, I ask more questions than the teacher can answer, but I do love it."

He played by himself at recess at first, since all the other pupils were white. When a marble championship was announced, however, George said, "I'll enter!" He won easily, and after that the students forgot about his color.

His life in Fort Scott was happy for a couple of years, but one day George saw a black man being

GUESS	1. pulled from jail.
	2. beaten on the head.
	3. burned to death.

George saw all this. He felt the hatred in the mob and heard their curses and their unkind remarks about blacks.

"I must leave here!" he decided. "I'm not wanted . . . but will I ever find another school?"

5

Schooling

Georgeorge wandered from town to town, but he did not forget the Carvers. He wrote a letter from Kansas: "I go to school until my money runs out. Then I work a while. Sometimes I start a grade in one city and finish it in another."

George worked

GUESS	1. sawing wood.
	2. racing cars.
	3. doing housework.

He sawed wood sometimes. Mostly, however, he did housework. People called him

GUESS	1. beautiful.
	2. cute.
	3. handsome.

People called him cute because of his merry heart and quick wit.

From Newton, Iowa, he wrote Aunt Mariah. "I'm working in a

greenhouse. I love it so much I think I'll stay here forever." But he soon moved because of

<table>
<tr><td rowspan="3">GUESS</td><td>1. the cold winters.</td></tr>
<tr><td>2. being called a thief.</td></tr>
<tr><td>3. the greenhouse burning.</td></tr>
</table>

The son of the manager said, "That George—he stole money from me."

George protested, "I didn't, I didn't!"

"Do you think I'd take your word instead of my son's?" The manager looked him in the eye. "You are fired! I'd advise you to get out of town."

George wandered south until he met a band of migrants going to New Mexico. "Could I join you?" he asked.

"Come along," they invited.

When George saw the desert, he threw up his arms and said, "How beautiful!" He drew a picture of a yucca plant on a piece of paper. "I'll keep this in my pocket always," he said.

He wrote to Uncle Andy from New Mexico, "I worked with the migrants for a while but stopped to go to school. I'm fifteen now and in the seventh grade. I bought me an accordion and learned to play. It helps me when I'm lonely. I think I'll go back north again."

Back in Kansas, he stopped at a place called Olathe. Here he met Mr. and Mrs. Seymour.

"Come stay with us," Lucy Seymour invited. "You can stay in school steady and share our home. You see, we have no children."

George noticed Lucy Seymour's smartly tailored black dress, which matched her black face. He observed her hair rolled into a large bun at her neck, with an enormous tortoise-shell comb atop her head. "Oh, ma'am," he said.

<table>
<tr><td rowspan="3">GUESS</td><td>1. "You look like a queen."</td></tr>
<tr><td>2. "Yes, I'll stay."</td></tr>
<tr><td>3. "No, I must keep moving."</td></tr>
</table>

George said, "I'll be glad to settle down with you Seymours."

When Lucy chided him about etiquette, he asked, "Why are you so set on good manners?"

"George, I was a slave before the war in the home of gentle Virginia landowners." Lucy lifted her head like a queen. "True gentlefolk are kind and considerate. If I don't teach you anything else, I'm going to teach you to be considerate, kind, and mannerly."

"Yes, ma'am," George said meekly.

But Lucy taught George more than manners. She taught him the art of fine

GUESS
1. music.
2. painting.
3. laundry.

George soon learned the difference between Aunt Mariah's "taking in washing" and Lucy Seymour's "fine laundry." Lucy bragged, "I'm the best shirt ironer and polisher in the country. Everyone says so. I do fancy ball dresses and can starch an undershirt so that it stands by itself."

When important people paraded in and out of the house, George remembered Aunt Mariah's saying, "It's not so much how much you do, but how well you do it." George wrote to her.

Soon he received a reply. Aunt Mariah said,

GUESS
1. "The Carvers are sick."
2. "Jim is dead."
3. "Uncle Andy cries."

The letter said, "George, your older brother, Jim, died of smallpox this past winter." Tears flooded George's eyes. He rushed outside and wandered over the fields. "I miss the woods at times like this," he murmured. "Where is the One who watches over me?" He threw himself down on the ground, beat it with his fists, and cried.

A red glow covered the sky, and the underside of the clouds caught the gleam. As George sat up, he prayed, "Oh, Jesus, keep Jim safe until I come to join You. Take my heart, Lord Jesus. I'm all Yours now." Streams of light burst through the clouds, seeming to surround George.

"Thank You, Jesus," he said.

When George returned home, Mr. Seymour took him into his arms, and Lucy put her arms around them both. No one said anything for a long time, but George felt their love and support.

Next day the three went

GUESS

1. to church.
2. to the fair.
3. to Neosho.

As they did every Sunday, the three went to the Presbyterian church. George watched the rays of the sun shining through the stained glass windows with a spectrum of red, blue, yellow, green. This Sunday he listened to the sermon—*really* listened. In his mind he saw Christ high and lifted up, reaching out to accept him. He saw himself going to Christ. When the preacher said, "Would you like to be a member of our church?" George

GUESS

1. refused.
2. joined.
3. waited.

George joined the church. Then the Seymours gave him a Bible of his own. "I'll carry it the rest of my life," he said. He wrote the date, September 25. "That's the date I really believed," he told Lucy.

He wrote to Aunt Mariah, "You tried to tell me about the salvation Christ gives. Now I know what you meant, for I believe."

The fall of 1880 the Seymours moved to the Salomon River Valley. George sent a letter to the Carvers. "I'm so glad to see more trees again. Here in Minneapolis, Kansas, there's a high school, but I still have to finish the eighth grade, you know."

He had learned the trade of finishing fine laundry so well from Lucy, that the Seymours agreed with him: "There is room in this city for

GUESS	1. another factory."
	2. another teacher."
	3. another laundry."

George started his own laundry in a one-room house with a lean-to kitchen on Main Street. He rented it for

GUESS	1. $10.00 per month.
	2. $5.00 per month.
	3. $25.00 per month.

As the rent was only $5.00 per month, George bought a stove, a boiler, tubs, washboard, rope, clothespins, soap, starch, blueing, an ironing board, a candle, and a couple of irons.

"You're getting ahead!" Lucy beamed, as business began to roll in. "Soon you'll be ready for high school."

All during his high school years, George operated his laundry. He sent the Carvers a copy of his day's activities.

> Work—4:00 A.M. until schooltime.
> School—9:00-4:00.
> Work until finished.
> When I fall into bed it is sometimes midnight.

"It will be worthwhile when you get into college, you'll see," Lucy told him.

Because he couldn't go places with other students, they

GUESS	1. left him out.
	2. went to the laundry.
	3. begged him to close shop.

Students drifted into the laundry. George told tales of his wanderings while the students watched him stir with a stick in his steaming boiler or rub the clothes in hot soapy suds. Friday nights he took time off and played his accordion for student get-togethers.

In high school there was another

GUESS
1. Lucy Seymour.
2. Moses Carver.
3. George Carver.

The principal discovered another George Carver and suggested, "Just use your middle initials to keep it straight."

The other George said his initial was V. The principal waited, pen poised to write. "Well?" he prompted.

The only thing George could think of after V was W, so he said, "W."

Later the other George teased, "What does W stand for? Washington?"

"Yes," George said and walked away. "I've learned not to let the white boys' teasing bother me," he told Lucy Seymour.

During all four years of high school, George worked on qualifying for college. Lucy kept saying, "Only a little more, George. I know you are tired, but stick to it. Only a little bit more!"

The students voted George the

GUESS
1. most intelligent.
2. hardest working.
3. best liked.

He was selected the Best Liked Boy, for he delighted everyone by his accordion playing for school marches.

After graduation in June 1885, he closed his laundry, bade the Seymours good-bye, and set off for Diamond Grove to visit the Carvers.

Uncle Moses grinned. "I'm proud of you. You can make money and lose it, but when you get an education, no one can take it from you."

"Are you sure you can get into college?" Aunt Susan asked.

George brought out his letter of acceptance from Highland College. "See,

GUESS
1. here's my name."
2. there's the president's name."

43

3. I'm already in!"

"I'm already accepted by the Reverend Duncan Brown, D.D. I'm already in!" George grinned. "Did you ever think your boy would go to college?"

6

Detour

That summer George grew to six feet. "It's all your good cooking, Aunt Susan!" George laughed.

He secured a job in Diamond Grove at the Union Depot. There he learned to operate the

1. typewriter.
2. telegraph.
3. computer.

George sent messages on the telegraph from 6:00 P.M. until midnight.

During the day, he farmed with Uncle Moses, who was now past seventy.

He gave money to the Carvers and the Watkins, so that when fall came, he had only enough money for his train ticket to Highland, Kansas.

He said,

GUESS
1. "I can't go."
2. "There is no way."
3. "I'll earn my way."

"No matter. I can always earn my way," he told the Watkinses and the Carvers, as they waited to say good-bye. "My wandering days are over. Now I'll go up, up, up!" He turned to Uncle Moses. "Remember my picture down by the creek? The one of the man climbing up to the temple of learning?"

"Yes." Both Aunt Susan and Uncle Moses nodded.

"Now I'm going to make it. My climb is almost over, and I'm about to enter the temple of learning."

"You deserve it," Uncle Andy said. "But *don't forget to give back to your people what you learn.*"

"I won't forget," George promised, as he kissed all his dear folk good-bye. Then he boarded the train amid cheers, tears, and prayers.

No one met him at the train station in Highland. A few questions, however, set him on the right path to the large red college building. George said, "It looks like

GUESS	1. a friendly place."
	2. the temple of learning."
	3. a prison."

George chuckled as he carried his cardboard suitcase. "It looks for all the world like the temple of learning in my picture." He hurried through the iron gates.

He strode down the long pathway to the pillared veranda, mounted the steps, and entered the lobby. He asked a red-haired lady at the front desk for Reverend Duncan Brown. She smiled at him and promised to watch his suitcase, as she pointed to an imposing office.

"Well, what do you want?" Mr. Brown said. "Can't you see I'm busy with the new students?"

"I know, sir," George said. "I'm one of your new students. Here. See me letter of acceptance."

Mr. Brown looked at the letter, then at George.

He said,

| GUESS | 1. "Welcome to Highland." |
| | 2. "You're on time." |

3. "You're a black."

"You didn't tell me you were black. We don't take blacks here." Then Mr. Brown turned, motioned another student into a side room, and shut the door.

Slowly George folded the letter, put it in his pocket, and left the room. He picked up his suitcase at the front door and walked out of the temple of learning.

As he went down the steps, the lady at the front desk called, "Wait a minute! Please!" She followed him to the bottom step. "I'm Mrs. Beeler, and I'm ashamed of what happened. Tears flowed down her cheeks. "I'm the one who checked your high school record and recommended you be accepted. Your qualifications are excellent."

George looked into her kindly white face and waited.

"If you will follow that road," she said, pointing to the east, "you will eventually come to a mailbox labeled 'Beeler.' Wait around there for me. My husband and I will try to help you."

George said,

GUESS

1. "I hate whites!"
2. "Leave me alone."
3. "I need a friend."

The look in Mrs. Beeler's eyes melted George's heart. "I need a friend," he said. "I'll go."

"And I'll be free in a few hours and will meet you at the mailbox," Mrs. Beeler said, as she held out her hand. George took it.

It was good that George had a long walk ahead of him, for his mind raced faster than his legs. George felt

GUESS

1. joy.
2. outrage.
3. disappointment.

Words of outrage and disappointment tumbled out as he

47

walked and talked to himself. It was only when he saw the mailbox with the word *Beeler* on it that he remembered Aunt Susan's words: "You can't help what *they* do—only what *you* do." Finally he prayed, "Oh, God, show me

GUESS	1. why I'm here."
---	2. what use I am."
	3. how I can get revenge."

George asked God, "Why am I here?"

By the time Mrs. Beeler rode up in her smart buggy, George's face was calm. By now he could hide his feelings. He even said, "Your fruit farm looks healthy."

After a good dinner, the three adults sat around a table in the fine dining room. Mr. Beeler raged angrily. "Kansas is a free state. We are supposed to treat everyone alike, but only in the Homestead Act is there equality."

"The Homestead Act—" George said. "I haven't heard of that. Tell me."

Mr. Beeler explained, "Our son has gone West and filed a claim on a hundred sixty acres of land. All he has to do is to build a house and outbuildings and farm it for four years. Then he can either own it or sell it."

"You mean it's

GUESS	1. expensive?"
---	2. cheap?"
	3. free?"

George gasped. "You mean it's free? For anybody, black or white?"

"Anybody who will stick it out and work hard."

"You don't need anything to start?"

"Well, no, but a mule, a plow, some tools, lumber, and supplies would certainly help."

George wrinkled his forehead and squinted his eyes.

"Tell you what," Mr. Beeler said. "You work around the fruit

48

farm this winter, and in the spring I'll see that you get the tools, supplies, and a legal claim near my son in Beeler."

Beeler was the name of

GUESS
1. the son.
2. the town.
3. the state.

A small town in the West was named Beeler after his son.

George agreed. "I'll work here all winter, if I can move to Beeler next year."

After a hard winter's work, the Beelers were true to their word to George. He set out in the spring of 1886 with a mule, a wagon, and supplies.

"God bless you on your trip," they said.

George had to get used to the grassy prairie of Kansas. "I see no hills, no rocks, no roads, and worst of all, no trees," he wrote to the Carvers. "I can look over the flat land for seven miles in any direction and see only buffalo grass, soap weed, tumble weeds, and the sky. I feel as though I never really saw the sky before, but the hundred sixty acres of land's all mine! Well, it will be, as soon as I've 'proved up' on it, of course."

'Proving up,' however, wasn't that easy. "First I need a house," he said. He made his hut of

GUESS
1. wood.
2. sod.
3. bricks.

George looked at the buildings of the other homesteaders and made his plans. With the mule and plow, he cut blocks of sod evenly into strips four inches thick and a foot wide. Then he cut the strips into two-foot lengths.

Sod is

1. clay.

GUESS

2. dirt held together by grass roots.

3. a kind of cement.

He set the thick sod blocks of dirt, filled with roots, in lines, making a hollow square. Carefully he laid another line of sod blocks on top of the first, like a row of bricks. He didn't work alone, for other homesteaders came to help. The Beelers' son, Tom, said, "I'll help every day until you finish."

Together they brought out a ridge pole and rafters from town. After they laid the boards across the top, Tom and George placed the sod to make the roof. Then they heaped dirt on top of that.

"It has to be a foot thick to keep in the heat," Tom cautioned. "Winters here are ferocious. When a blizzard comes, you'll even have to place hairy animal skins over the oilskin windows to keep out

GUESS

1. wild animals."

2. the snow."

3. the cold."

"The skins will keep out the cold," Tom said.

After everyone was gone, George raked off the roof so that it was smooth and neat. Then he trimmed the inside walls with a sharp spade and white-washed them with lime. He built crude furniture, and the last of his money went for a pot-bellied stove with a flat top.

"I'll cook and heat with the same stove," he decided. Finally he sat down. "Well, here I am, twenty-two years old and sitting in my own little soddy." He sighed. "I feel like Moses before he saw the burning bush. Will I ever get any more education? Should I give up all hope for college? Oh, God, help me!"

7

Poetry, Music, and Painting

George plowed the Kansas prairie and planted his precious seeds. "The spring is lovely. My seeds are sprouted, and stalks of corn grow taller and taller," he wrote to the Carvers. "I work hard hoeing and nurturing my vegetable garden." He stopped writing to look at the sunset. *If this garden doesn't produce soon, I'll be out of food,* he thought.

Then the hot winds came. They brought

GUESS	1. no rain.
	2. no shade.
	3. no heat.

For weeks on end the winds blew without a sign of rain. *I was never in such a place,* George thought. *There's no shade and no escape from the boiling sun or wind.* All his plants wilted to the ground. Even his mule sickened and eventually died. He slept outside on the open ground, for his soddy was like an oven.

Other homesteaders also suffered. Only the cattle ranchers could survive. The owner of a livestock ranch next to George's place offered George work, and he thankfully accepted. "I must have money for food," he said. He also had to prepare for winter by

GUESS

1. gathering cow dung.
2. gathering buffalo dung.
3. chopping trees.

"Gather all the buffalo chips you can find, and you're welcome to cow dung from my lot," the rancher said. "Winters here are cold, and there isn't much fuel beside sunflower stalks and what cornstalks you have left. It takes a lot of chips, believe me!"

So every day George scoured his land for buffalo chips. Without the mule, he had to pull them in the wagon himself.

This takes a strong back, he thought.

When winter came, George found himself snowed in for days. When he pushed on his door, he only found a solid bank of snow. Anyone else would have been lonely, but George occupied himself by

GUESS

1. playing cards.
2. memorizing poetry.
3. studying spiders.

George memorized poems.

He also made a study of spiders, since the little creatures had discovered his warm shack in a bitter cold world. Their webs so inspired him that he copied their patterns and made lace. He also had time for reading his Bible and praying. During these long days of silence, except for the crackling of the fire, George learned to talk with God. "Only with His help did I keep my sanity," he said later.

Then George decided to write a poem himself:

The rich and poor, the great and small
By God's same sickle all must fall
Each moment is golden and none to waste
Arouse thee then, to duty haste.

O' sit not down nor idly stand
There's plenty to do on every hand.
If you cannot prosper in work like some,
You've at least one talent, improve that one.

He knew his one talent was painting. He soon covered the whitewashed walls with vines and flowers. He experimented with paints made from weeds and sunflowers. Some faded quickly; others stayed bright. When he could, he bought a few sheets of drawing paper in town.

On George's land there was an odd-shaped mound. He examined it over and over. "There is something under that ground, I know. Something is swelling and wants to get out."

The something was

GUESS	1. treasure.
	2. oil.
	3. a monster.

Years later oil was discovered on that very spot, but George didn't know anything about oil when he lived there. After two miserable years of fighting the weather George was offered $300 for his homestead. He accepted.

Then George walked

GUESS	1. east.
	2. west.
	3. north.

George walked north and crossed into Iowa. "Oh, God, how good the trees look. How wonderful to see rivers and greenery again," he said aloud. The gentle breeze comforted him.

"If I see an opportunity, I stop and earn money scrubbing clothes or doing chores," he wrote to Aunt Mariah.

Not far from Des Moines, he found a green and peaceful village called Winterset. *What a charming place!* he thought, as he walked down the main street.

He saw a sign in the window of the Schultz Hotel that read, "Cook Wanted." George went inside. He liked Mr. Schultz at once. The man's voice was deep and commanding with a German accent. *Just like Moses Carver's,* he thought.

"Now you understand," Mr. Schultz said, "we serve elegant meals. Not like a greasy spoon."

"I understand," George answered, remembering his success with Mr. Payne, who wanted his food just so. "I will surprise you with my cooking. I know how to prepare . . ." And George named the dishes he had learned from Mrs. Payne.

Mr. Schultz responded,

GUESS

1. "So you say."
2. "I'll test you."
3. "You're hired."

"You're hired," Mr. Schultz said. "Sunday is your day off, because we have businessmen who go home weekends." He showed him the cook's quarters and introduced him to the kitchen and the helpers.

From the beginning George liked the small town. When Sunday came, he worshiped with the local Baptist congregation, as there was no Presbyterian church. "Doesn't matter that much," George decided. "God is here, too." Since he was the only black person present, everyone noticed him when he came in and quietly sat down.

He sang the hymns with the congregation and enjoyed the church choir, especially the soloist, Mrs. John Millholland. He didn't know it, but he was sitting next to

GUESS

1. Mr. John Millholland.
2. the preacher.
3. the president.

Mr. Millholland listened to George sing.

When the preacher began his sermon, George opened his Bible to the text. He bowed his head during prayer.

After the service several people spoke to George briefly, and the preacher shook his hand. "Welcome. Please come back. We hope you'll like our church."

George was walking down the church steps when Mr. and Mrs. Millholland stopped him and introduced themselves.

"Would you come visit us this afternoon?" Mrs. Millholland invited.

Everyone noticed George.

George looked at them sharply, but they seemed sincere. "Yes, I could come around two, if you tell me where you live." He smiled. "I'm new here, you know."

Before two o'clock George followed their directions and passed the house several times. He saw a beautiful home, with a large porch and neat lawn. "They invited me. Why do I feel I should go to the back door?" he asked himself. "I wonder what they want —must be something." Out of curiosity he finally walked to the front door and knocked.

The door opened and Mr. Millholland said,

GUESS	1. "Go to the back door."
	2. "Please come in."
	3. "I don't know you."

Mr. Millholland smiled. "I'm so glad you came. Please come in."

They seated George in the best parlor, served punch and cookies, and asked about his job at the hotel. Soon Mr. Millholland told about his conversion, and George answered by explaining how he accepted Christ.

George was polite and called them Mr. Millholland and Mrs. Millholland.

"Oh, for pity sakes!" the wife suddenly exclaimed. "I'm Jill, and he's John. Don't you understand we want to be friends? May we call you by your first name?"

"Of course. It's George."

"Let's sing," Jill suggested, going to the piano and playing a hymn.

John and George joined her, and the house soon rang with their voices. George relaxed and began to enjoy the visit.

"I have some special music in the study," Jill said. "Let's all go in there." The three walked down the hall and entered the study.

George stood spellbound before

GUESS	1. a carved desk.
	2. a typewriter.
	3. an easel.

"You paint?" George asked, looking at the half-finished picture on the easel.

"I try!" Jill answered.

George saw the stiff and stilted flowers and the garish colors.

"Look, the center of your picture is too far away. Your color needs attention. See, like this." George

GUESS

1. pointed at her picture.
2. painted over her picture.
3. slapped paint everywhere.

George picked up the brush and painted swiftly. It was the first time he had used oil paints, but he had no trouble.

Jill watched in astonishment. "You—you really do know how to paint. The flowers do look better. How did you learn?"

"By practice, by looking at living flowers. Of course, I don't know all the rules of painting."

"Would you give me lessons?" Jill asked. She looked at him questioningly. "And I'll give you singing lessons. That would be fair, wouldn't it? And, oh, George, would you, would you *please* sing in the church choir? We need a tenor!"

8

The Burning Bush

Soon George was in and out of the Millholland home every day. Along with singing lessons he learned to play the piano. Jill insisted he play by notes, though he was able to pick out the tune by the sounds. This helped

GUESS

1. his painting.
2. his singing.
3. his poetry.

Knowing the musical notes helped his singing as well as his piano playing. There was a piano at the hotel, and George played whenever he could get away from the kitchen. Soon people stopped by. "We want to hear George play," they said. For over a year he led a happy life in Winterset haunted only by thoughts of college.

All the time George was on the Kansas prairie he had looked for a "burning bush," like Moses of the Bible—some sign from God as to what he should do. When his "sign" came, it was not in the form of a burning bush, but a

1. teacher.

2. preacher.

3. college freshman.

The Millhollands were always inviting weekend guests to stay in their home. One day George met a fresh-faced young man who was their visitor.

"Glad to know you, Larry." George smiled. "Are you in high school?"

"Oh, no," Larry answered. "I graduated in June. I've just started Simpson College in Indianola, Iowa."

"I once dreamed of college—was even accepted for the freshman class." George could talk about it now, for the hurt had faded if not gone.

"Oh, what happened?"

"When I arrived, they saw I was black and told me I could not enroll."

"*What!*" Larry objected. "We had one black student at Simpson a few years ago."

George looked at the white boy. "You mean it—a student black like me?"

"Yes, of course," Larry agreed. "If you have a high school certificate, you could come back with me. It's not too late to enroll for the fall term."

George said,

| GUESS |

1. "I'll have to pray about it."

2. "I'll go."

3. "I'd have to quit my job."

George gazed for several minutes at the young student. He breathed a silent prayer and said, "I'll go."

In a flurry George quit his job, collected his things, and said good-bye to good friends. Jill and John forced some clothes and supplies upon him, and before he knew it George was enrolling at Simpson College.

"You will have to be a special student," Dr. Holmes, president of the school, said. "You haven't had enough mathematics."

George paid his twelve dollars tuition. He didn't tell anyone he only had

GUESS

1. ten cents left.
2. two dollars left.
3. ten dollars left.

He had only ten cents left.

"Our dormitories are only for white students," Dr. Holmes said apologetically. "The other black student lived in town with his parents. Let me see—there's an old abandoned shack that belongs to the college. I guess you could stay there until you can find a place. Sorry, but it's the best I can do on such short notice."

Dr. Holmes sent a student with George to show him the building, which was

GUESS

1. close to the college.
2. a long way.
3. many miles away.

The shack was several miles from the college, but it was stout and free, so George didn't complain. First he cleaned it. He slept on the floor. "I'll have to build myself a bed soon—and find some way to heat this place. It's already September and getting cold."

The next day he found a store and bought five cents' worth of suet and five cents' worth of cornmeal. "Enough food for a week." He decided, "First thing to do is

GUESS

1. start classes."
2. start my fine laundry."
3. cook breakfast."

"First I must get my laundry started," he said. He went to the junkyard and searched until he found a small stove with three legs. It was flat on top. "Just right for a boiler!" he exclaimed.

"You need a boiler?" the junk dealer quizzed him.

"Yes."

"Well, I've got an old beat-up one—copper even. Someone threw it away. You can have that."

George promised to pay the small amount for the stove as soon as his laundry prospered.

"No hurry," the man said. "It's doing me no good. Been setting there a year anyways."

On the way home with the stove, George saw a black pan that had been tossed into an ash can. "Someone'd rather throw it away than to clean it." He laughed. "I'll have me a nice pan in no time."

Still he needed more supplies, and he gritted his teeth as he went to a store and asked the owner for credit to buy two wash tubs, a washboard, irons, soap, and starch. He used wooden boxes for a table and chairs. Finally he was ready.

Dr. Holmes promised to announce the laundry to the students. George hoped he wouldn't forget.

Dr. Holmes

GUESS	1. told all the faculty and students.
	2. forgot about George's laundry.
	3. went away.

School absorbed George's attention once he started classes. He asked to take painting. "You have a heavy schedule already. Are you sure you need painting, too?" the registrar demanded. George insisted.

"Tell you what," the woman said, "you go to Miss Budd's introductory class for two weeks. She can test your talent. Then we'll decide about the class. Fair enough?"

"Sounds fair to me," George agreed, eager to paint for Miss Budd. But when class started, he saw Miss Budd draw

GUESS	1. outlines.
	2. stick figures.
	3. curved lines.

He saw her draw stick figures on the blackboard.

"Everyone draw a stick man, standing, sitting, walking." She droned on and on.

By the second week she let them make balloon figures, as George called them. He obediently followed her directions and drew ovals, wondering when they would ever paint anything. "How can she find out if I have any talent if I never do anything?" he asked himself.

At the back of the room he noticed Alice from an advanced class. She was trying to paint

GUESS

1. lilies.
2. dandelions.
3. roses.

When Miss Budd gave the class a break and left the room, George walked back to Alice. "I see you are painting roses," he said.

"Glad you recognize them. They are such a mess." George could see she was about to cry.

"Here, let me help you," he took her brush, and with quick sure strokes he corrected the painting. "You have too many petals. No rose ever grows that many. And here—the stem goes this way. The leaves grow thus."

In a short time the red blotches came alive under George's hands.

"Here comes Miss Budd!" someone warned, and the pupils all scurried back to their desks and their balloon figures.

When Miss Budd entered, she started to walk past Alice. Then she

GUESS

1. stopped.
2. patted Alice on the head.
3. stared in surprise.

"Well, I do believe you are getting the idea at last. I've never seen such improvement," she said.

Alice grinned. "Thank you, Miss Budd, but I didn't do it."

"Who, then?"

"George—George Carver."

It was as though Miss Budd were seeing George for the first time. "Please stay after class," she said to him.

When the class ended, George paused. Standing first on one foot and then the other, he waited.

"Well, George." Miss Budd smiled as she said,

GUESS	1. "Why did you paint?"
	2. "You are experienced."
	3. "You have talent."

"I see you do have talent," she said. "You may go ahead and sign up for my other class. The advanced class. Pay your fee, and I'll expect you at three o'clock tomorrow."

George stopped smiling. "The fee?" he asked weakly.

"Yes, there is an extra charge for painting instruction. Didn't you know?"

"No," George answered.

"There's a problem?" Miss Budd seemed concerned.

"You see, Miss Budd—" George swallowed. "I've started a laundry, but no customers have come. Dr. Holmes must not have told the students, as he promised."

Miss Budd said,

GUESS	1. "Dr. Holmes never forgets."
	2. "He probably forgot."
	3. "He's absentminded."

"He probably forgot. He's absentminded, you know," Miss Budd said. "If it's money you need, my friend Mrs. Liston has begged me to send someone to paint the flowers in her garden. Since I had no one qualified, I sent no one. But you are gifted, and she will pay you well."

George's eyes lit up. "You mean I'd make money painting? I never expected that."

"Nor I. This is unusual, and temporary." Miss Budd laughed.

When Mrs. Liston found out that George had not eaten for two days, she paid him in advance. Not only that, she looked around for a good place for a laundry.

"You live too far away from your customers," she noted. "Main Street is more convenient for both students and Indianola townspeople."

Later she found George painting in her garden. She said, "I've located a small shop. You have painted so many lovely pictures of my garden, I'm giving you a bonus of

GUESS	1. a million dollars."
	2. a paint set."
	3. a month's rent."

"I'm giving you a month's rent," Mrs. Liston said.

With the help of several students, George moved his laundry tubs, the stove, and other equipment to the shop on Main Street.

"It's beginning to look like Lucy Seymour's laundry," he told them.

"What are you going to do for heat at your place, since you moved the stove over here?" one student inquired.

"I'll worry about that when I start making money." George could laugh since he had seen so many hard times. But the other students murmured among themselves. George saw them lift their eyebrows and wink.

So many people brought their laundry that George was busy every spare moment. He propped up a book on the stove warmer and stirred clothes in his boiler while studying. He read while rubbing the clothes on the scrub board. Many students came to bring laundry and stayed to hear of George's wanderings.

One day George came home tired. "I believe I can afford a stove soon," he told himself. "Thanksgiving is coming, along with Old Man Winter."

He lit a candle as he entered the shack and saw

GUESS	1. a bear.
	2. a tank.
	3. a new home.

George saw his home transformed—a bed, table, chairs, dresser, and a shiny stove with a fire burning.

The next day he asked everyone, "Who did this?"

Everyone answered, "Not me. Not me."

9

Changes

Toward the end of the school year, Miss Budd said, "George, please stay after class."

Once the room was empty of students, George walked past the desks and stood before Miss Budd.

"You have passed all your classes and made us proud of you. Tell me how you feel about your year here at Simpson," she said. "No, don't stand there—sit here!" She indicated an empty chair beside her desk. "Now, how are you feeling about things?"

George answered,

GUESS

1. "I'm happy here."
2. "I hate school."
3. "Everyone is mean."

George smiled at his friend. "Miss Budd, I'm happy here. You folks have made me feel like I count for something, like a human being. I guess I loved painting the flowers most of all."

"Yes, I know you did, and you paint well, but you'll never be able to make a living painting!"

George replied,

1. "Oh, yes I will."

| GUESS | 2. "I'm afraid you are right."
3. "I can always scrub clothes." |

"I'm afraid you are right," George replied, hanging his head. "But I can't give it up!"

"Don't give it up," Miss Budd hurried to assure him. "Paint for pleasure, but make a living with your second love."

"My second love? What's that? Not scrubbing clothes, I hope."

"Your love of nature. You couldn't paint the way you do if you had not observed how plants grow. How they flower. How they produce seeds. Your paintings show your love for living things."

"That's true, Miss Budd," George said. "I'm surprised you know that about me. My happiest hours are spent in the woods. Several students go with me every Saturday."

"I know. I've heard." Miss Budd smiled. "I also heard about your singing in the church choir—and about the offer of a scholarship to sing at the Boston Conservatory of Music. Why didn't you take it, George?"

George answered,

| GUESS | 1. "I can't be bothered."
2. "I don't like singing."
3. "Singing won't help my people." |

"I don't know how to say it, Miss Budd." George hesitated. "I like singing, but that won't help my people much."

"So, what you really want is to help your people?" Miss Budd gazed into George's brown eyes. "Is that right?"

"Yes," George gulped. "I have God's work to do. I have my people to serve."

"George," Miss Budd spoke earnestly, "my father is a scientist. He is a professor at Iowa State Agriculture College. Suppose I write to him about you?"

"About me!" George gasped.

"Yes, about you. As a scientist in the field of agriculture, you could

1. get rich."

67

| GUESS |

2. serve your people."
3. be popular."

Miss Budd said, "You could serve your people!"

Letters flew back and forth, and by September 1890, George received a scholarship to Iowa State Agriculture College in Ames. He arrived there on time.

The registration clerk said to George, "Professor Wallace, your botany teacher, will be your adviser."

George stood awkwardly in the huge hallway, several cards in hand.

What shall I do? he wondered, looking at the crowds of young people hurrying from table to table. Finally his eyes settled on a cardboard sign over one table—*Professor Wallace.*

Oh, yes, he's my adviser. Well, I do need advice, George reminded himself. He stood in line and listened to the students ahead of him. He began to understand the procedure.

"Name?" the professor said, as George approached.

"George Carver."

"Oh, yes, here we are." The professor explained

1. the course of study.
2. about his dog.
3. how to find classes.

After explaining about classes, Professor Wallace ended with, "Now, your dormitory room is—What?" The professor stood up in alarm.

"Wait a minute," he said to George and left the crowds of students to storm into the president's private office.

Students behind George complained,

| GUESS |

1. "Where did he go?"
2. "Is he coming back?"
3. "Why did he leave?"

The students complained about the professor's absence, but

everyone waited until he returned.

With a red face, the teacher motioned George into a long hallway. Names were printed on all the polished doors.

"Here. See this one that says James Wilson?" Professor Wallace opened the door. "Sit here until Professor Wilson comes! He will help you finish."

George sat as asked. He looked at the large empty desk, the empty shelves and bookcases. He said,

| GUESS | 1. "James Wilson must be a ghost!"
2. "No one lives here."
3. "There is no James Wilson." |

George muttered to himself, "I see no one lives here."

Much later, Professor Wilson introduced himself. "Sorry you had to wait so long. There was a mix-up about your room. No, George, I'll be honest. There wasn't a mix-up. Every dormitory has refused to take a black man."

"No matter, sir," George interrupted, grateful for the kind eyes looking at him. "I didn't stay in the dormitory at Simpson, either. They had an old shack I stayed in."

"You'll not stay in a shack here!" Professor Wilson's eyes snapped. "This will be your room. I have a small office upstairs and didn't want to move down here anyway. Now you have the finest dormitory room in the college—and at no cost, either." He waved George aside when he tried to object.

"Your bed is coming, and I've ordered a wardrobe for your clothes. The bathroom is down the hall."

George surveyed the room with new eyes. "But, it has a soft carpet, beautiful drapes, such a desk as I've never seen." George stopped in amazement as the door burst open and workers entered with furniture.

"Come, George, let me help you finish your registration."

After Professor Wilson conducted George about the campus, George said, "I can find my way around now." Thankfully he returned with the professor to his room.

When George walked in, he saw

1. nice furniture.

| GUESS |
2. dinner on the table.

3. a radiator with steam heat.

George saw the furniture and steam radiator. He saw that someone had brought his trunk from the station.

"Thank you, Professor Wilson." George's eyes showed his gratitude. "Believe me, I'll study very hard to be worthy of all this!" The two shook hands, thus beginning a lifelong friendship.

George loved all his classes but one, speech class. He repeated, "How now brown cow," and, "Peter Piper . . ." until he could say them perfectly, but the teacher was not satisfied.

"Of all the ridiculous voices I ever heard, none is as bad as yours." He directed George to

| GUESS |
1. put pebbles in his mouth.

2. recite rhymes.

3. lower his tones.

By the end of the semester, George was happy to find out he had passed. The teacher said, "You'll never have really low tones, but at least you have acheived a balance that is bearable."

George wrote to Aunt Mariah, "At last I found someone who can answer all my questions. Now I know where the sun goes, why the flowers have different colors, and what happens to the fluff of the milkweed."

He also wrote to Miss Budd and Mrs. Liston. "I have fun joshing with the help in the kitchen, where I take my meals. Their jokes tickle my funny bone."

One day Mrs. Liston arrived unexpectedly. "Are you surprised to see me?" She laughed in George's face.

"You didn't say you were coming, but I'll be glad to show you around. Can you stay for dinner?"

"Oh, yes, indeed. One of the things I wouldn't miss. I want to hear the funny jokes of the kitchen help."

George wondered

| GUESS |
1. why her eyes twinkled.

2. why she smiled like a cat.

3. why she cried.

George wondered why she grinned like a cat.

When they entered the dining hall, the director greeted them. "Oh, Mrs. Liston, we are happy and honored to have you as a guest today." He bowed, ignoring George completely. "Where can I seat you?"

"Oh, I'm eating in the kitchen with the help." Mrs. Liston grinned. "You see, I came to Iowa State as a guest of George Carver. I expect to be treated as he is treated."

The manager's face fell for a minute. He sputtered,

GUESS	1. "But, but madam!"
	2. "What will the dean say?"
	3. "Very well."

When he recovered, he said, "I see, but what will the dean say?" He paused, looked around, and went on, "I see. Well, George is now assigned to table number six with the other students. You can both sit there."

For four years George Carver sat at table six. Soon students begged to be assigned to his table. It was the one filled with the loudest laughter and the most interesting conversation.

George's college days were full. He studied

GUESS	1. plant chemistry.
	2. rules of botany.
	3. how to heal sick plants.

George learned all these things, along with experimenting with bacteria living on plants. He wrote to Aunt Mariah, "I'm learning a million things I didn't even know I didn't know. Someday I hope to find a use for it."

10
Awards

When Christmas vacation came, George stayed at the college, while the other students went home. "If I went home, I'd go to

GUESS

1. the Carvers in Diamond Grove."
2. the Watkinses in Neosho."
3. the Seymours in Minneapolis."
4. the Millhollands in Winterset."

George thought about it. "All four couples gave me a home at different times. I love them all and must send them something for Christmas."

George sent each couple

GUESS

1. a box of candy.
2. a Christmas card.
3. a box of snow.

George took out his paints for the first time at the college. After he painted a winter scene and made up a verse for the inside page of his Christmas cards, the thrill of painting came over him again.

"I'll spend my vacation painting," he said happily.

He painted two pictures, one of roses, one of lilies. Then he started hunting. "Somewhere I have a sketch of a yucca plant," he mumbled, throwing his things about.

Finally he pulled out the faded and much folded picture he had sketched so long ago. *I'll have to be careful with it,* he thought. *It's about to fall apart.*

Once again he seemed to see the New Mexico landscape. The yucca plant danced before his eyes and came alive on his canvas. "Best painting I ever did." He smiled in satisfaction.

When the students returned, they asked George,

GUESS	1. "What did you do?"
	2. "Weren't you lonesome?"
	3. "Did you set off firecrackers?

"Weren't you lonesome during vacation?" the boys at table six inquired.

The one called Bill said, "I thought of you on Christmas Day, all alone here at the college. I felt sorry I hadn't asked you to come home with me."

"Don't be sorry for me." George laughed. "I had a wonderful time painting pictures."

"You paint? I didn't know that. Can we see the pictures?" his friends clamored.

So the six boys of table six trooped to George's room. They thought the pictures were

GUESS	1. good.
	2. bad.
	3. horrible.

"Oh! Ah! How great!" they exclaimed. "You must enter them in the fair this spring."

Heavy studying soon claimed Geroge's attention, but his

friends remembered his paintings and insisted he enter the competition.

"You will surely win!" they agreed.

"Oh, I doubt that," George replied.

All five boys joined George after school the day of the judging. Together they hurried to the fairgrounds. "You'll win!" they kept assuring the doubtful George.

Someone produced a ticket for George, and the gang pushed through the crowds to the Exhibit Building. Hurrying past the cattle, jellies, and quilts, they finally came to the paintings.

George had won

GUESS	1. first prize.
---	2. second prize.
	3. third prize.

The young men held George up. His legs felt like they had turned to water.

"I can't believe it, I can't," he said, but there was the blue ribbon on his yucca plant, a red ribbon attached to his roses, and a white ribbon on the lilies.

Even his friends gasped. "You won *all* the prizes!" They examined the other paintings. "Don't even come close to yours," they decided.

Together the friends celebrated and laid plans. "Now we'll enter your pictures in the All Iowa State Fair of 1892," Bill insisted.

Professor Wilson passed the boys as they ate hot dogs, laughed, and shoved each other.

"Oh, ho! I see you have our hero here!" he greeted them. "Congratulations, George. Table six has won again."

"We don't deserve the credit!" Bill exploded. "It's George Washington Carver all the way!"

"Seriously," Dr. Wilson said, "George is probably the very finest painter in the state of Iowa."

"And we aim to prove it," Jim and Jack said together.

Bill added, "We are entering his paintings in the

1. State Fair."

74

| GUESS |

2. Chicago Fair."

3. Paris Fair."

"We are entering the paintings in the State Fair," Bill added.

"See that George goes with them to the art exhibit in Cedar Rapids!" Professor Wilson added.

"Oh, I couldn't," George objected. "I have no proper clothes, no ticket, no money. But send the paintings, if you like."

All six young men came to George's room and helped frame the bulky pictures and pack them.

"You are right. They do look better with frames," George admitted. On their way to the post office together, George said, "The Fair is in May, so they'll get there in plenty of time."

A few days before the Fair, four boys beat on George's door.

"Whatever are you doing?" George exclaimed, recognizing his friends from table six. "I was just changing from my National Guard uniform to my work clothes. I have a job cleaning Miss Perkins's basement this afternoon."

"We know all about that!" Bill interrupted. "Jake's gone out there to clean it. You are coming with us!"

"Now? Why?" George didn't move.

Two boys stepped to each side of George. Grasping him under his armpits, they

| GUESS |

1. beat him.

2. lifted him.

3. threw him down.

They lifted him bodily and carried him down the long hall and outside to a waiting carriage.

"Where are we going?" George gasped, as he struggled to free himself.

"You'll see!" Bill looked mysterious. "First we are going to Main Street."

No one would reveal more, though George pleaded with them all the way to a men's store.

In the store Bill said, "We want

75

GUESS
1. jewels."
2. hats."
3. suits."

"We want the finest suit you have for this young man," Bill told the clerk.

No objection of George's stopped the boys. Soon he stood in front of a mirror in a brown tweed suit.

"I hardly recognize myself," George said. "You know I seldom wear a white shirt and a tie. What's this about, anyway?"

In a few minutes he found himself at the train station, holding a leather suitcase and a ticket to Cedar Rapids.

As the train pulled in, his friends told him, "You are going to the State Fair to see the Art Exhibit. All arrangements have been made—your hotel, your meals—and here is money for a carriage and such."

George was too weak with surprise to refuse the money Bill thrust into his pocket.

With tears in his eyes, George waved to his friends through the train window. "Thank You, Lord Jesus, for friends." George rejoiced. "I don't deserve them."

Upon George's return, the same friends met the train. "How did you come out?" they demanded.

George reported,

GUESS
1. "I lost."
2. "I won."
3. "I don't know."

"The yucca plant won first place, and the lilies, honorable mention," George reported. "Oh, thank you for sending me! I had a wonderful experience!"

Difficult classroom work claimed George at once. He had to make up the assignments he had missed and keep up with his work as a soldier in the National Guard.

"Did you know our guard unit was selected by Governor Boies to march with him at the World's Fair?" Bill asked.

"No, really!" George gasped. "I wonder if they will want me along, my black face being so different."

"I don't see why not," Bill countered, "but we can ask General Lewis, if it will make you feel better."

The two friends walked together across the green campus to the guard headquarters. "We're lucky. General Lewis just came out the door," Bill said.

"Oh, General, we have a question," Bill announced.

The general stopped in his tracks. "Yes?"

Bill explained George's doubts about being included in the battalion.

General Lewis said,

GUESS	1. "You are out of place."
	2. "We want you."
	3. "You're not worthy."

"George—" General Lewis put his hands on George's shoulders "—you have overcome your poor posture. You have mastered every skill and passed every test. You have the rank of lieutenant and will probably be captain by the time we reach Chicago. Why do you doubt you will be included? We want you, George Carver!"

"Well, sir—" George hesitated "—we know that no matter what rank I get in the college National Guard, I'd not be allowed in the regular Army."

"It is a good thing that's true, George. I hear of your good work in agriculture. I hear you are becoming an outstanding scientist. You are needed in that field. But as for marching at the World's Fair, yes, you will march with us in Chicago."

But when the time came,

GUESS	1. George was sick.
	2. he failed.
	3. he marched.

George marched with the governor of Iowa.

He thought as he viewed the vast crowds, *I feel like I'm a black man marching in a white man's world.*

He was prouder, however, when he visited the Art Exhibit.

The Iowa State Fair Committee had sent his picture of the yucca plant to the World Competition.

Breathlessly George entered the building with Bill. "It's so big. Do you think we can ever find it?"

"Over here, this way, down the hall." Bill led the way.

"There it is, George Carver. See it?" Bill pointed with glee.

There stood the yucca painting with

GUESS	1. a disqualification.
	2. a ribbon.
	3. a black mark.

A ribbon was attached. It said, "Honorable Mention."

"Honorable mention among the painters of the whole world." George gasped. *I guess that proves a black man can do anything a white man can do,* he thought.

11

What Use Is It?

"I wonder what I'll do after graduation," George said to himself, as he studied for his final exams. He looked around his room. "They have been wonderful to me here, giving me this room and all. But I wonder what good will come of it!"

Just then his eye fell on a bookmark that said,

GUESS	1. "Poverty overtakes laziness."
	2. "Live up to responsibility."
	3. "Seek God first."

George remembered the bookmark. "I got it at a YMCA banquet in Ames." He looked at it closely and read, "Seek ye first the kingdom of God, and all these things shall be added unto you. Matthew 6:33."

George made up his mind. "That's what I'll do."

"Graduation is almost here," George wrote to Jill and John Millholland. "I'm the first black to graduate, though there was another who started here. I like our class motto, Ever Climbing, because, though I've learned a lot, it has opened up so many new fields. I see I have a lot more to learn. I wish I could stay here."

George folded the letter and put it in an envelope with a sigh. *I should be thankful for this much schooling and not ask for more,* he told himself firmly. *After all, I'm thirty years old.*

Behind a curtain with other students, George put on his graduation cap and gown. Everyone was peeking out into the audience to see parents and friends. George did not peek, because

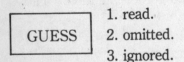

1. he was ashamed of Aunt Mariah and Uncle Andy.
2. none of his loved ones came.
3. he didn't expect anyone.

Though George expected no one, when the class filed out onto the platform, he spotted Miss Budd and Mrs. Liston near the back. He could not help grinning at the surprise.

Bill pinched him and whispered, "You're supposed to be solemn."

After a long speech the college president read out the names of those in the top 10 percent of the class. George Carver's name was

GUESS

1. read.
2. omitted.
3. ignored.

I hope Miss Budd hears my name, George thought. *I did study mighty hard to get to the top.*

Awards were made, and people recognized. *It gets rather long,* George was thinking, as he stirred restlessly and looked at the strained faces around him. Suddenly, he jerked to attention. What was the president saying? "In special recognition of excellence in agricultural research, a scholarship is awarded to *George Washington Carver* to study

GUESS

1. in Paris."
2. in New York."
3. in Iowa."

George's scholarship was to study further at Iowa State.

Stiffly, George managed to climb the steps to the president and nod his thanks as he took the precious scholarship paper. He never knew how he got back to his seat or managed to accept his diploma.

"I'm staying! I'm learning more!" he babbled to Miss Budd when the ceremony was over.

The two white women hugged him. "You deserve the chance," Miss Budd said.

"Do a good job! Remember the job you do is a self-portrait," Mrs. Liston advised, as she directed George to the lunchroom.

As they finished their lunch, Professor Wilson joined them. "Your job as a graduate student will be that of assistant botanist in the Agricultural Experimental Station, and you will be in charge of the greenhouse," Professor Wilson explained.

"Oh, Professor Wilson, you are the best boss in the world." George looked into his eyes. "You have already taught me so much. I'll look forward to learning more. As for the greenhouse, you know it is my first love."

In the days that followed, George not only listened to Professor Wilson in class; he also attended his Sunday afternoon Bible discussions. George and Professor Wilson soon got a reputation. "Those two

GUESS	1. are flower fanatics."
	2. carry their Bibles."
	3. love insects."

People said of the two, "They carry the Bible in their hearts, not merely under their arms."

During 1895 George wrote a paper called "Plants as Modified by Man."

"You see, Henry," he told his twelve-year-old greenhouse helper, "God created plants, but we can make them

GUESS	1. weaker or stronger."
	2. taller or shorter."
	3. have more or less flowers."

George looked at his young friend. "We can do all those things and also cross them with other plants to make a new kind."

Henry Wallace, son of the director of the Experimental Station, stared at George with his blue eyes. "Oh, sir, show me how to do it."

George winked at him. "When I was your age, I, too, wanted to know, but there was no one to teach me."

"How did you learn then?" Henry asked.

"I walked in the woods every morning at four A.M. I looked at the things God made and studied them. When I came here, I got more answers. Your daddy showed me how to test the soil, how to know which plants grew best on different soil, and how to find out the chemicals in every plant."

"Can you show me?" Henry's yellow hair bounced.

George held the boy by both shoulders. "Henry Wallace, you shall know all you can learn right here in this greenhouse."

Wherever George walked, Henry was behind him. Together they planted, nourished, and coaxed the plants. As they worked, Henry asked questions, and George answered.

Other people asked,

GUESS	1. "Isn't Henry a nuisance?"
	2. "Doesn't he bother you?"
	3. "Aren't you tired of questions?"

"No, Henry Wallace reminds me of myself," George said. "I'll always have time for his questions."

Early every morning the two walked together over the Iowa countryside. They saw farms with

GUESS	1. solid houses.
	2. strong silos.
	3. painted barns and silos.

George admired the stout Iowa farm homes, the painted barns, the strong silos, and the well-fed cattle.

Henry pointed. "See the hogs and turkeys and chickens!"

"Oh, sir, show me how to do it."

"Notice, too, the machines for doing field work," George pointed out. "That work was done in the South by slaves not too long ago."

"Were you a slave, George?" Henry dared ask.

"No, but my mother was," George admitted.

"Are you going to the Exposition in Atlanta?" Henry asked. "Father says the South has come back, and President Cleveland will sit on the platform with a black man."

George stopped walking. "You mean it? I'll talk to your father right away."

Professor Wallace invited George to go with him to Atlanta. Together they inspected the Negro Building. It was

GUESS
1. designed by blacks.
2. built by blacks.
3. filled with exhibits.

"All this was done by the blacks of the South," Professor Wallace said. "But now we must hurry to hear the speeches."

George noticed several black faces in the audience but only one on the platform.

"Who is that sitting next to President Cleveland?" George asked.

"That's

GUESS
1. Will Rogers."
2. Booker T. Washington."
3. Teddy Roosevelt."

"That's Booker T. Washington, principal of Tuskegee Normal and Industrial School in Alabama. Sh! It's starting."

Governor Bullock of Georgia gave the opening address, and Bishop Nelson, President of the Exposition, welcomed the people to the Exposition. The crowd stirred. George waited patiently. Finally Booker T. Washington rose to speak.

"I see a ship lost at sea," he began. "The people are thirsty, having used all the water on board. Finally they sight another ship, and cry out, 'Water, water, please, water!' The men on the second ship call back, 'Cast down your buckets!' But the people continue to cry, 'Water, oh please, water.' 'Cast down your buckets,' they are told over and over. At last someone on the lost ship ties a rope around the handle and lowers a bucket into the sea. To everyone's amazement, fresh water from the mouth of the Amazon River is brought up."

George listened to the speech. He was

GUESS	1. spellbound.
	2. angry.
	3. touched.

"I see it all," George told Professor Wallace on the train racing back to Iowa. "I'm touched that the Negroes of the South need to reach down where they are and pull themselves up from poverty."

"It's not that easy," Professor Wallace said. "Someone must show them *how.*"

"Booker T. Washington is trying to do that. Don't you see?"

"Yes, but he is only one. What can he do alone?"

When the two stepped off the train, a group of athletes met them.

"Oh, come quick, Mr. Carver,

GUESS	1. the dorm is on fire."
	2. the pipes are frozen."
	3. our basketball player is hurt."

"Our best basketball player has sprained something and is screaming in pain," they cried.

George hurried to the side of the athlete. Blending some herbs with tallow, he rubbed the player's arms and legs, as Aunt Susan had rubbed him when he was a boy.

"He's stopped screaming." The boys in the hall comforted each other. "I wonder what magic that George Carver has in his long fingers that he can soothe bruises so."

Early in 1896 George got a typewritten letter. It was from

GUESS

1. President Cleveland.
2. Henry Wallace.
3. Booker T. Washington.

The letter read, "I'm speaking in Cedar Rapids, Iowa. Please meet me there." It was signed, "Booker T. Washington."

At the meeting Booker invited George to come and work at Tuskegee Institute. "You are the man for the work. You are the only black who really understands agricultural research. I can only offer you a thousand dollars a year, but I can offer you a chance to help our people."

Aunt Mariah's very words, George thought. *I'll go!*

12

Tuskegee

"**B**ut we need you here!" Professor Wilson objected. "Where can we ever find a man who has collected over twenty thousand specimens of fungi, as you have?" He looked around the greenhouse. "You

> **GUESS**
>
> 1. understand soil."
> 2. are expert in crossbreeding plants."
> 3. have been to the moon."

Professor Wilson admired George's understanding of soils and plants.

"It will be impossible to fill your place. Please reconsider. We can pay you fifteen hundred dollars a year—and board!"

"Dear professor, you are kind," George answered, "but I take this as a call from God to serve my people in the South."

Professor Wilson relented. "Well, I will never part from any student with so much regret."

The most difficult good-bye George said was to

1. old Henry Wallace.

GUESS 2. Professor Wilson.

3. young Henry Wallace.

George hugged young Henry. "Don't forget God or your old friend. We both love you," he said.

The faculty held a farewell banquet and gave George a gift. It was a

GUESS 1. suit of clothes.

2. a microscope.

3. a greenhouse.

George said, "All that I am, I owe to this place and to all of you. For that reason, more than for this gift of a microscope, I thank you."

He continued his speech. "No one has a right to come into this world and to go out without leaving behind him a reason for passing through." He paused. "I pray my work at Tuskegee will become my reason for living."

October 10, 1896, George Carver boarded the train bound for Alabama. He wore his brown tweed suit. It was faded now to an odd gray color, but George wore it proudly. He waved at a station full of people—students, faculty, workers. Sitting on his father's shoulders, Henry Wallace waved wildly.

George watched out the window. Through tears, he saw

GUESS 1. old shacks.

2. splendid farms.

3. good roads.

"Iowa is a place of prosperous farms and good roads," he noted.

He slept fitfully overnight and changed trains next morning. "You! Go to the last car!" he was ordered. "We've passed the Mason-Dixon line."

"I had almost forgotten," George apologized, walking to the

rear of the train. Here, he sat with the black folks. Flies buzzed. Many people hugged crates of chickens or ducks.

"Are you a farmer?" he asked the man sitting next to him.

"Reckon I am," the man replied. "I know all there is to know about farming. I've wore out

GUESS

1. two farms."
2. three farms."
3. five farms."

"I've wore out three farms in my lifetime," the old man explained.

"How?"

"Why with cotton, naturally. I farm the land till it don't make no more cotton, then I moves on to the next farm."

"And the land is washed into deep gullies," George observed, "like I see out the window."

"Yes, that ain't proper land no more."

George looked at the barren fields, some still producing a few straggling cotton plants.

As the train drew closer to Alabama, he saw more

GUESS

1. miserable shacks.
2. happy people.
3. sagging fences.

George gulped as he saw the gullied fields, straggling fences, unpainted shacks. He saw thousands of acres of cotton, growing to the very doors of the shacks. "The roofs are torn, the chimneys sag, and there's not a tree, flower, or vegetable garden in sight," he gasped. "I see it is

GUESS

1. impossible."
2. a circle."
3. square."

I see it is a circle, George thought. *I can help my people only by healing their sick land, and I can only heal the land through the people. It goes round and round.*

"The people picking cotton look whipped by life," George muttered. He gazed at their thin bodies covered with shreds of overalls. "Those in the towns don't look any better. The women are wearing dresses made from feed bags. I see no beauty, no comfort."

When he saw a group laughing, he asked the farmer about them.

"They laugh to keep from crying," the farmer said sourly.

At a train stop, George slipped off the train for a few minutes and collected an armload of Alabama plant life. When he sat back in his seat, he held up a plant.

"What's this?" he asked the farmer.

"Them's all weeds."

"But every weed has a name and a purpose," George protested.

"I don't know no name or no reason for weeds." The farmer turned away. "They makes us chop the cotton, that's all."

"Chehau, Chehau," the conductor called.

"This is where I get off," George said, as he collected his things. He jumped to the platform when the train stopped. His trunk was dumped beside him, and he looked around as the train pulled off, belching steam.

George saw

GUESS

1. no one.
2. a boy and a buggy.
3. a crowd.

George saw no one at the station. Going inside, he noticed an old sleepy gentleman settling down for another nap.

Just then a horse and buggy whipped up beside the station. A young black man stepped out.

"Seen a gentleman? A Mr. Carver?" he asked, looking at George in his battered old cap, his baggy gray-brown suit, and his high-laced shoes.

"I'm Mr. Carver," George said.

"Oh," the young man said, "I'm sorry I'm late. That's a nice flower in your lapel. Dr. Washington is expecting you, sir." He helped George load his trunk and bags into the buggy.

As they rode the three miles to Tuskegee, George quizzed the young man. "What's your name?"

"Jim Hardy."

"Tell me, Jim, about the students here."

"We are all poor and have to work our way. Everyone learns some trade."

"Like what?" George prodded.

"Like building wagons, making harnesses, saddles, shoes, mattresses, brooms—" Jim paused. "Oh, and the girls do laundry and cook."

"How long does it take to graduate, since you do all this work?"

"Oh," Jim answered,

GUESS	1. "four years."
	2. "six years."
	3. "seven or eight years."

"Takes most seven to eight years."

"How about farming?" George asked.

"Farming! Are you kidding?" Jim stopped himself. "Sorry, sir, I shouldn't have said that, but our folks been farming for years and years. We want none of that cotton picking!"

"What do you want to study?"

"Latin and Greek. We want to learn to be fine ladies and gentlemen, not farmers like slaves," he said.

When they drove up to a four-story brick building, with shacks scattered about, Jim stopped.

"This is it?" George gasped. "This is Tuskegee Institute?"

Booker T. Washington rushed out of the building. "Welcome, welcome to Tuskegee!" He beamed. "See our brick building. We call it Alabama Hall. I want you to know the students made the bricks, laid them, and finished everything themselves!"

"It does look good," George said with more appreciation than he felt.

As they ate dinner together, George admired

GUESS

1. the efficiency.
2. the good manners.
3. the lace tablecloths.

"I admire your efficiency in the dining hall and the good manners of the students," George said.

"Don't expect too much of us," Dr. Washington warned. "We are poor in everything but spirit."

After the meal, they took a walk. "I want to show you the Agriculture Building."

"I'd like to see it," George said, thinking, *It must be invisible, since I can see at a glance that nothing is here but this one building.*

When George saw it, he was

GUESS

1. surprised.
2. upset.
3. disappointed.

Booker took him some distance, on the way pointing out the Department of Dairy Science, which was a churn under a tree. The Animal Department consisted of one yoke of oxen, a few sheep, a few cows, and thirty razorback hogs.

Booker beamed. "The sheep give us wool to weave."

In hot Alabama? George thought, holding his tongue.

"This is the Dairy Department," Booker said, pointing to a few scraggly cows. "The cows give the students good milk, and the hogs furnish meat. We also have a plow, a wagon, and a team of horses."

"I see," George said.

"Here we are," Dr. Washington pointed out. "Here is the Agriculture Building on top of the hill overlooking our farm land."

George could see

1. 2,000 acres of poor land.

GUESS

2. shifting sands.
3. gullies.

"I don't see the building," George said. "I only see sand and gullies."

"Oh, the building is now on paper only. But we have collected $10,000 to build it, and the students have started making bricks already."

George swallowed. He dared not ask how long it would take to build it.

"And the laboratory?" he asked.

"Your department exists only on paper, Carver. And your laboratory will have to be in your head for now."

"What of laboratory equipment?" George asked. "You can do nothing without equipment."

"The equipment has to be in the head of the man and not in the laboratory. Be patient, please," Dr. Washington said. "Your main problem, Carver, is not equipment or buildings. It is

GUESS

1. power."
2. students."
3. drugs."

"It is students. Only thirteen have signed up."

"Only thirteen want to be farmers?" George asked. "You have over a thousand students."

"Don't ever say *farming*, Carver. Say *agriculture*, or you will have no students. Your task here is to teach them there is as much dignity in tilling a field as in writing a poem."

"I'll begin where I am. I'll do with what I have." George bowed his head. "Through Christ, which strengtheneth me."

13

Beginnings

At 4:00 A.M. George Carver rose, as he always did. "I do wish I had room to unpack my trunk," he said, as he looked around his cubbyhole. "But the bed takes almost all the room."

Later, a student brought a bowl of warm water, but George was far away by then.

He followed the road back toward the

<table>
<tr><td rowspan="3">GUESS</td><td>1. woods.</td></tr>
<tr><td>2. bridge.</td></tr>
<tr><td>3. city dump.</td></tr>
</table>

He walked toward the city dump, observing his fields. "That gully is large enough to drop a wagon and team of horses into. The soil is clay underneath and sandy on top." He spoke aloud, for he was not alone. Every morning, he walked and talked with God.

When he reached the dump, he said, "Everything we need is here."

He observed the swampy wasteland that existed in the area. "Good, good." He rubbed his hands in glee. Then he noticed

1. morning glories.

GUESS

2. tin cans.

3. a pumpkin plant.

He saw a pumpkin plant growing in a tin can, and he plucked a piece of the vine before heading back to the campus for breakfast.

"This is your classroom, Professor Carver," a respectful student guide pointed out. "And here are your students, thirteen, I believe."

George entered the classroom. The students saw a thirty-three year old, tall, lean young man, whose shoulders stooped when he forgot to hold them straight. He had a handle-bar mustache, the style of the day, and a soft smile.

George grinned. "We have an adventure before us," he said. "See this vine, full bodied, rich, healthy, strong. I picked it this morning. Can anyone guess where?"

"You didn't find it on campus," Jacob Jones declared.

"Why not?" George asked.

"There's nothing growing on our two thousand acres but scraggly bushes and tumbleweeds. Nothing that looks like that, green and healthy."

"You are right," George admitted sadly. "I call our land 'the big hungry,' and we are going to feed it. Help it recover from its sickness until it can produce a healthy plant like this!" He held up the pumpkin vine.

"How can we do it?" John Palmer asked.

George then poured out his heart, teaching his students about the elements in soils. He ended by saying, "After dinner, come back here, and I'll take you to

GUESS

1. the sun."

2. the moon."

3. where plants grow."

"We'll go where the pumpkin vines grow, where we will get food for our soil, equipment for our laboratory. Everything we need to give 'big hungry' a square meal."

Later George brought the wagon and horses around to the classroom. The students climbed aboard, laughing and joking.

"We're off to find treasure! Will we have to dig for it? Or climb? Or dive?"

"You'll see." George only smiled. But when he stopped the horses at the city dump, the students held their noses. "Phew! It smells! Treasure, me eye!" The students sat still.

"Out of the wagon," George directed. "I want to show you something."

Reluctantly the students dragged themselves to his side. George took them deeper into the dump. They all stepped gingerly around the garbage.

"There it is," George said in his high, squeaky voice. "See the

GUESS	1. sunshine."
	2. pumpkin vine."
	3. flowers."

The students stared at the pumpkin wine, with seven runners nearly forty feet long, loaded with big, healthy pumpkins.

"Pick them gently, boys, we'll have pumpkin pies for dinner."

As the young men loaded the wagon, George said, "This morning I told you the soil needed fourteen elements to be healthy. Where will we get them?"

Jacob and John stopped. "In the

GUESS	1. creek."
	2. dump."
	3. tin cans."

Jacob answered, "In the dump?"

John said, "You mean in the garbage?"

George smiled. "How clever you are. Of course, it wasn't the tin cans that nourished the pumpkin plant, but the garbage. Once we have plowed our fields, we will mix in the garbage."

The other students gulped. "Garbage! Garbage! How icky, how sticky, how revolting!"

George just smiled. "Come, I have something else to show you." He directed them to the

96

GUESS	1. skyscrapers.
	2. city.
	3. swamp.

The students followed George to the swamp. "These lands extend for almost three miles. What kind of plants grow here?"

"Rich, green plants. But no wonder, they are sunk in water!"

"And

GUESS	1. muck."
	2. slop."
	3. black soil."

George pointed out, "That muck, as you call it, is good black soil, soil full of every element we need."

"Won't help us," John objected. "It's here, and we are way over there."

"We could move it," Jacob offered.

After everyone laughed, George said, "Yes, we could move some of it. Wouldn't be easy, but it is the medicine our sick land needs. I once wrote a poem:

'O' sit not down nor idly stand
There's plenty to do on every hand.'

"I never saw a place where there was so much to do!" George added.

The students agreed.

"But we can't move the swamp soil or the garbage today. Actually, we need to plow deep into our soil first to mix

GUESS	1. clay."
	2. flour."
	3. dust."

"We need to get as much clay mixed into the sand as possible," George said.

"Then we can mix in the garbage and the muck," Jack added.

"What can we do today?" John asked.

"Today, we begin the most important part of our work. We start our laboratory."

"A laboratory? Who needs a laboratory?" Jacob sniffed.

"We do!" George said emphatically. "First of all to test our soil to see what elements we have and—more important—to find out what we don't have."

The students looked about helplessly.

George picked up a broken bottle. "See this. It is a glass beaker. We will need many of these!"

John picked up an old ink bottle. "This any good?"

"Yes, with a wick, that will be a Bunsen burner. We will need about fifteen of those."

"How about this chipped teacup?" John laughed.

"That's a mortar bowl. We will crush dirt and other things in it. We'll need a few dozen."

Soon all the students were holding up "finds." Fruit jar lids. "To hold chemicals." A flat iron. "To pound things." A tin can with holes. "A good sifter." Reeds from the swamp as a substitute for glass tubes. George found a use for almost everything, and slowly the students filled the wagon.

They all walked home, jabbering about their treasure hunt.

Soon the students built

GUESS	1. hen houses.
	2. cattle sheds.
	3. shelves.

They first built shelves in their classroom, since there was no other place for the laboratory. Slowly things took shape, and classwork progressed.

Booker kept giving George projects he considered agriculture. "Care for the animals. Do the dairy work. Fix the fences. Fix the plumbing. Do the landscaping of the campus."

Patiently George dealt with these everyday problems. "It has to be done," George said, casting a longing eye at his laboratory.

One day George's students grinned broadly as he took his seat behind his desk. George looked down and saw a bug.

"What have we here?" He smiled.

He examined it carefully, noting the body of a beetle, legs of a spider, and the head of a great ant.

"What bug is that?" the students asked, as soberly as they could. "You told us to bring plants or insects to class to identify. What's that?"

George looked at the class gravely. "Oh, that, my young gentlemen, is

GUESS	1. a spider." 2. a beetle." 3. a humbug."

"That's a humbug," the professor announced.

By the end of the first school year, seventy-six students had enrolled in Agriculture, and thirty-six in Dairy.

In another year, the Agriculture Building was actually completed by the work of the students. Booker T. Washington invited two governors, a dozen mayors, judges, teachers, and reporters to the dedication.

"Is there anyone you would like to invite?" the director asked George.

"Yes, I'd like to ask my old teacher at Iowa State, James G. Wilson."

"Very well," Booker agreed.

The day of the dedication dawned with fair weather.

"It's well," Booker said. "The audience is so large, at least

GUESS	1. one thousand." 2. three thousand." 3. five thousand."

"We could never get five thousand inside," Booker said. "Oh, by the way, has your teacher arrived yet?"

"Yes, where do you want him to sit?" George asked.

"We have so many important people on the platform. Would he mind sitting in the audience?"

"I don't think so, but shouldn't someone introduce him?" George asked.

"Why?" Booker asked. "He isn't important."

"He is! He is

 GUESS

1. President of the U.S."
2. U.S. Secretary of Agriculture."
3. head of a department."

"He left Iowa State last year to become U.S. Secretary of Agriculture in Washington, D.C.," George explained.

"What! And we didn't ask him to speak?" Booker hurried to make a place on the platform and to rearrange the program.

When George was asked to say a few words at the dedication, he said, "We are sinning against the land. It is washed out and eroded. We are not protecting it, and in turn it is punishing us. The land our students nourished—that land you can see from here —produced twenty-pound cabbages and onions seven inches in diameter this year. If you feed your hungry soil, it will feed you."

The farmers in the audience stared at George in

GUESS

1. anger.
2. disbelief.
3. scorn.

Until the farmers saw the cabbages and onions, they could not believe. *How long, O Lord, how long will it take for them to feed their land?* George wondered.

100

14

Money

"**G**eorge Carver, you are the most exasperating teacher in this school," the school treasurer scolded.

"Why, what did I do?" George looked up from his microscope. He had been alone in the laboratory, testing, experimenting—happy.

"It's not what you do, it's what you don't do. You don't

GUESS

1. come to meals."
2. cash your checks."
3. comb your hair."

"Look here," the treasurer said. "Here are three checks. They've been lying in my drawer waiting for you to pick up for the longest time. And now it's another month."

"What do you want me to do?" Carver looked innocently at the man.

"Here, sign all four checks *now*. I brought my cash box, so I can give you the cash. And from now on, come to my office the first of every month, and pick up your pay."

"Yes, sir," George replied, anxious to get on with his research.

As the teasurer shut the door, he mumbled, "He says, 'Yes, sir,' but he'll

GUESS

1. demand his pay early."
2. forget, as usual."
3. never get paid."

The treasurer mumbled, "He'll forget, as usual, and I'll have to track him down. What a man. No interest in money at all."

If George was not interested in money, others were. Booker T. Washington spoke to him one day. "You know the school is having financial trouble, and you can help out."

"Me?" Carver looked surprised. "What can I do?"

"You can

GUESS

1. paint."
2. play the piano."
3. research."

"Every Sunday afternoon you play the piano for the students and faculty. You know, just before you teach your Bible class."

"Yes."

"Well, we could arrange for you to have concerts in churches this summer during vacation time. Would you agree?"

"If that's what you want of me." George laughed. "I do love playing the piano, but I didn't know I was that good."

"Then it's agreed. I'll have

GUESS

1. a car ready."
2. a suit made."
3. a parachute ready."

"You can't wear that old brown tweed. I'll have a suit made for you. Tell me, why does that suit never wear out? It was old when you came here."

"Very simple. I've mastered the art of re-weaving. When an elbow or knee wears out, I simply take the threads from someplace else. I guess you've noticed I no longer have cuffs. I weave the cloth back in."

"Oh, what will we do with you?" Washington laughed. "Anyway, I'll get you an outfit for the concerts."

George was thunderstuck when he saw the clothes. They were

GUESS
1. a full dress cutaway.
2. a vest.
3. gray walking trousers.

"You expect me to wear a full dress cutaway?" He gasped. "Me, George Washington Carver, the scientist?"

"It will be expected. You are playing in large churches in Montgomery, Savannah, and Baton Rouge."

"I don't know why I ever agreed to this in the first place!" George declared.

But he wore the suit and made the tour during July and August 1899. He came back five weeks later with

GUESS
1. $1000.
2. $500.
3. $350.

"Here is three hundred fifty dollars," George told the treasurer. "That is the total of the offerings."

He presented Booker T. Washington with a box. "Here is my cutaway suit with the vest and gray pants. I will never, never wear them again. Please don't ask me. This is the end of my career as a piano player."

"Except for playing here at the school."

"Except at school, of course."

"Don't downgrade yourself," Booker pleaded. "You were good. We got excellent reports. There are simply a limited number of people who attend piano concerts, that's all."

"I'm glad school is starting. I'm at home with the students and in the laboratory. That's where I belong."

On registration day, George happened to be in the office when a big powerful black boy walked in.

"What is your name?" the registrar asked.

"Tom Campbell."

"We don't seem to have a reservation for a Tom Campbell," the clerk wavered. "Where is your letter of acceptance?"

"Don't have any!"

"Well, then we may not have room. We already have more students accepted than we can afford."

Tom's face fell.

George stepped to his side. "Come into this office, and let's talk about it." He smiled and led the way.

Once they were seated, George said, "Now tell me your story."

"I walked all the way from Georgia to get here. I heard this was a place to learn," Tom said. "I even lied and stole food to make it here in time."

"What do you wish to study?" George asked.

"I don't know!"

"Farming?" George inquired.

"No! Absolutely not! I been farming all my life!"

George smiled. "How about

GUESS	1. music?" 2. art?" 3. agriculture?"

"Yeh, agriculture sounds good. I'd like that fine."

"Tell you what. Here's fifty dollars for the entrance fee. You go out and stand in line. By the time you get to the desk, I'll have your reservation ready."

"Thank you, sir. I didn't know you had to have fifty dollars. I thought the school was free. Honest, I did."

"It is free, in that you can work for your board and room. Just keep things honest, you hear! No more lies, even for a good cause!" George patted Tom's back. He didn't feel right, reaching up to pat his head.

One day after classes had begun, George came to his classroom early to finish some research. He was out of sight, behind a screen, when Tom and several students arrived.

Tom spoke his mind. "That Carver, he makes you want to learn."

"He never pretends he knows something when he doesn't," Harry Palmer added. "He just says he'll find out, and he does. Believe you me, he does."

"Yeh, but you better not start something and not finish it. He hates quitters," Andy said.

"I heard him tell Jim last year, 'I will help you while you progress, but once you quit, I will not waste my own time further.'"

"Last year he told me, 'Don't take up my time with

1. facts.'"
2. questions.'"
3. excuses.'"

" 'All I want is the thing done. Don't take up my time with excuses,' he says."

"And Tom," Jacob said, "never use the word 'about.' Professor Carver will tell you, 'If a ditch is five feet wide, and you jump *about* five feet, you'll fall into the water.'"

"That's right. He says there are only two ways to do something, and *about* is always the wrong way. Give him exact measurements every time."

The talk about the teacher ceased when George walked from behind the screen and took his place in front of his embarrassed class.

"Today, I want to talk about a trinity," he said, drawing a triangle on the blackboard. "At each point we can place something that makes the whole. At the top, soil." He wrote the word. "Second, plants, and on the third point,

GUESS

1. man."
2. animals."
3. stars."

George placed the word *man* on the third point and continued his lecture. "We must master a knowledge of all three. Now we have improved our soil here at the school by planting

1. cowpeas."

GUESS   2. cotton."

3. tobacco."

"We have planted cowpeas, which put nitrogen into the soil and made it rich. We have improved the soil and produced outstanding crops—peanuts, cowpeas, cantaloupe, watermelon, onions, and potatoes—plants of many kinds." He pointed to the word *plants*.

"Why have we worked so hard at this?"

Tom spoke up. "To show them hard-headed farmers you have to put something back in the land. You can't plant cotton on and on, year after year. Take, take, take, and never give back anything."

"Exactly!" George grinned. "And how can we get the message to *man*?" He pointed to the third angle.

"We can show them our fields!" Harry suggested.

"We can send out bulletins!" Jacob said.

"What if they can't read? What if they can't come? Them farmers in Georgia ain't coming this far!" Tom exploded. "You got to go to them! You got to show 'em!"

George learned from his students. He wrote a

1. letter.

GUESS   2. bulletin.

3. book.

He wrote a bulletin about cowpeas and a book about nature.

"Cowpeas are good food for man and beast," he proclaimed.

George made up eighteen recipes for cooking cowpeas and put them in the leaflet. The students printed and addressed the bulletins to every farm address they could find.

George talked to Booker T. Washington. "How about a

 1. party?"

GUESS   2. show?"

3. Institute for Farmers?"

George asked for an Institute for Farmers and their wives.

"Let them come here and get one day of school a month all year long."

"Go ahead." The director smiled. "Every third Tuesday in the month."

The students watched as every imaginable kind of wagon arrived. They welcomed the farmers and took them to the fields. There the men pulled up the potatoes to see the size, handled the onions, and felt the cabbages. The pupils told of swamp muck, compost, and the cowpeas.

"You see the rich soil. It was nothing but sand not long ago," the students said.

Later the students talked to George. "Only seventy-five farmers came, out of so many."

"That's all right," George said. "It only takes a little yeast to raise a loaf of bread. Don't you know they'll tell their friends, and then more will come?"

Through the years

```
GUESS
```
1. thousands came.
2. a few came.
3. no one came.

In later years, thousands of farmers visited Tuskegee.

One day George and Tom Campbell left the campus. Behind their horses they dragged a three-story wagon. "Do you think it will tip over?" Tom asked.

"Oh, no. I've got the cow on one end and the razorback hog on the other."

When they parked their wagon beside a church or on a town square, everyone came to see the exhibits, from food to needlework. They learned rug making, caring for the sick, food preparation, and how to make and apply whitewash.

George taught them, "Learn to live at home. Don't spend your money at stores. Plant vegetables, can fruits, make pickles. Learn to make your own shoes. Live well on your own farms."

At the end of the day George and Tom were weary. "What difference will it make?" Tom asked.

107

15

Peanuts

"**N**obody will really believe you, about your soil, I mean, till you show them how much cotton you can grow," Tom Campbell told George one day.

"All right, our soil is rich now. We will plant an acre of cotton and see how much we get," George agreed.

That year, they raised

| GUESS | 1. one hundred pounds.
2. three hundred pounds.
3. five hundred pounds. |

The students raised five hundred pounds of cotton on an acre of land and grew fifty bushels of peanuts an acre. This was news. The reporters came, took pictures, and the white farmers said, "Can't be. We've been raising cotton for years and never came near that amount."

When they finally dragged themselves to the "all black school" to see for themselves, George told them, "Cotton is killing the South. It is taking life from the land. We will always be poor, as long as cotton is king. Plant peanuts instead."

But it wasn't George Carver who overruled King Cotton. It was

GUESS	1. lice.
	2. the boll weevil.
	3. storms.

George told the farmers, "The Mexican boll weevil is heading our way. He is now eating through Louisiana and Mississippi. Once he gets here, there will be little left for our farmers. Plant peanuts, plant sweet potatoes."

But George Carver was really upset one day when he and Tom Campbell were out with the exhibit wagon. A little, old, toothless black lady sought him out.

"I believed you, sir, when you said to plant peanuts. I got a bumper crop and took them to town to sell," she said. "Sir,

GUESS	1. no one would buy them."
	2. thieves stole every one."
	3. the wagon tipped over."

"George Carver," she said, with tears in her eyes, "what use is it to grow tons of peanuts, if no one will buy them?"

George went back to Tuskegee

GUESS	1. discouraged.
	2. angry.
	3. resolved.

George stormed into the office of Booker T. Washington. "I need a well-equipped laboratory, so that I can find uses for peanuts. Then my farmers can sell them to industry. I've been here twelve years. When I came, you asked me to be patient about getting a laboratory. I have been patient! I have worked with every makeshift thing imaginable. Now I want my lab. I need my lab desperately!"

But Booker said, "I want you to make records of rainfall, report the weather, start a chicken ranch, put in plumbing throughout the campus, and produce clear, clean water for the students. You can

109

do all that without a laboratory—or at least without a new lab."

"I see there are two jobs here. Why not put my assistant in charge of the things you mentioned?"

"Very well, *he* will be the new Director of Agriculture, and *you* can be his assistant."

"Never! He is a good man but has no knowledge of research. I cannot work for him." George walked out.

George went to his room and pulled out letters from his desk. "I have all these offers to teach in white schools, which pay large salaries. They will give me every type of equipment and all the laboratory space I need. Everything! And I've never considered saying, 'Yes.' " George knelt beside his bed. "Oh, God, what would you have me do?"

The next day George heard a knock on his door. When he opened it, he saw

<table>
<tr><td rowspan="3">GUESS</td><td>1. his assistant.</td></tr>
<tr><td>2. Booker T. Washington.</td></tr>
<tr><td>3. Teddy Roosevelt.</td></tr>
</table>

"Come in, Booker," George said. "What do you have in mind?"

"Let's have two departments. Let your assistant run the Agriculture Department, and you be the Director of Research."

"And a new lab?"

"You can have it soon as it can be built."

"And I can do research alone? No classes?"

"As you like," Booker agreed. "We will even give you a raise in salary to one hundred twenty-five dollars a month."

"No need of that. What would I do with more money?" George hesitated. "One thing, though. If I should die, will the school give me a Christian burial?"

"Of course. How strange! I didn't know you were concerned. Don't you feel well?"

"I feel fine. I just want to put my mind at rest."

Everyone was happy with the new arrangement, except the

<table>
<tr><td rowspan="2">GUESS</td><td>1. assistant.</td></tr>
<tr><td>2. reporters.</td></tr>
</table>

3. students.

The students howled, "You can't take Professor Carver away from us. No one else teaches as he does."
Finally George agree to

GUESS

1. teach again.
2. take field trips.
3. hold farmers' classes.

The students won, and George continued with a few classes.
Work on the laboratory began at once. It was completed in 1909.
First, George made black paint from

GUESS

1. sand.
2. soot.
3. clay.

It was made from soot from coal-burning furnaces. Before this, the soot was thrown away. He invented so many things using waste products that people from all over the country came to see George Carver.
One day he opened his door and saw

GUESS

1. Booker T. Washington.
2. Teddy Roosevelt.
3. Henry Ford.

"I'm Teddy Roosevelt." A large hairy man beamed at the thin, stooped scientist.
"The President of the United States!" George gasped. "However did you hear of me?"
"Oh, little birdies tell me things." Teddy winked, as he moved

his large bulk into the lab. "I hear you call this 'God's Little Workshop.' "

He sat on a stool. It was the only seat in the lab, since George stood while working.

"Now tell me of your accomplishments, yours and God's. I promise to shut my big mouth for once!"

"Well, first, we made black paint from soot. Then with paint on my mind, I went for a walk early one morning. The sun shone on a clay bank as though God was telling me to test it. We made three hundred products from clay. Whitewash to brighten up Negro cabins, cellars, stables, barns, henhouses, even pigstyes. Yellow wash for buildings." George paused. "And the bluest paint since the Egyptians.

"You see, sir, the lab is not just to analyze but to make new. God gives me the inspiration."

"Go on. I know there's more!" the President prodded.

"Yes, I don't know where to begin. Anything will give up its secrets if you love it enough." George frowned. "Oh, yes, we—God and I—developed a dust to kill the Colorado beetle on white potatoes. Also, a bedbug exterminator that does not stain, a coffee substitute, and syrup from sweet potatoes."

"And—go on."

"Oh, yes, our boys strung wires for electricity at Tuskegee long before they had electric lights in town." George paused.

"And the peanut," Teddy Roosevelt said. "Tell me what you made from the peanut!"

    1. linoleum, meal, ink, bleach, synthetic rubber
    2. paper, instant coffee, rubbing oil, plastics
GUESS   3. chili sauce, shampoo, wood filler, mixed pickles
    4. shaving cream, axle grease, washing powder
    5. salve, metal polish, a dozen different drinks

"With companies making *all those things from the peanut,* southern farmers should be able to sell all they can raise," President Roosevelt said. "You will be rich and famous."

George looked the President in the eye. "I don't ask for money or fame. I ask that black people improve and be respected."

16

Fulfillment

People kept coming to George's door. The men representing the manufacturers wanted him to tell them

GUESS

1. how to get to the moon.
2. how to fly.
3. how to make products.

"Now, what we want to know," one said, "is how you make linoleum from peanuts."

"And how do you make such beautiful marble from sawdust?" another asked.

Still another inquired, "We make cough syrup. We hear you have a cure for breathing troubles made from creosote. We will pay you well, if you tell us!"

"I'll tell you all, gladly, I will, but I'll take no pay. God never charges for His work. Neither can I in working with Him. Someone sent me a hundred dollars once, but I sent it back."

A dye plant sent a man from the north to get George's formula for blue color made from clay.

"Your blue is seventy times bluer than blue!" the representative said.

"Yes, I know. The ancient Egyptians used it to decorate their tombs. It has been unknown ever since."

The representatives begged him, "Help us put all five hundred thirty-six of your dyes on the market."

"No, no, no," he cried. "I'm not here to help rich companies but to help the man furthest down. Take the formula, but do not use my name!"

When war came in 1917, it brought a food shortage. George went to Washington to put on a demonstration before

GUESS

1. army bakers.
2. food experts.
3. congressmen.

In a demonstration kitchen, army bakers and agricultural experts watched George bake bread made of sweet potato flour.

"It is delicious. Best substitute for wheat flour we've seen," they declared.

He also demonstrated "egg yolks," tapioca breakfast food, syrup, vinegar, and alcohol made from sweet potatoes.

Thomas Edison sent his assistant to Tuskegee to offer George a job in his laboratory; the salary would have been $100,000 a year.

A great rubber company also offered a high salary.

But George said, "No, oh, no. If I go, my people would get no credit for my work. I feel if I should work for money, God's help and inspiration would leave me. I belong here."

In 1921 a messenger appeared on George's doorstep. He wanted George to

GUESS

1. come see a sick cow.
2. help a woman with her roses.
3. speak before the U.S. Congress.

"The peanut farmers of the South are in trouble. Companies buy peanuts from other countries, instead of from the southland," the messenger said. "Please come to Washington! We have arranged for you to speak for twenty minutes before the U.S. Congress."

"But why?" George stared blankly. "Why me?"

"You can convince the congressmen to vote for the Hawley-Smoot Bill, which will keep foreign peanuts out. Then the companies will buy from the southern farmer again."

"Very well. When shall I come?"

"On January 20," the messenger replied.

As George was packing his samples in two wooden boxes, Booker T. Washington opened his door. "Here is a new

GUESS	1. suit."
	2. tie."
	3. overcoat."

Booker held out a tie for George to wear on his trip.

"Do you think a new necktie will help me answer the congressmen's questions any better?" George laughed. "I prefer the tie I made and dyed with my own dyes."

"You do? And I suppose you are wearing that old suit, the one that used to be brown."

"Of course! That's my good suit! The faculty and students of Iowa State gave it to me to wear to the Fair in 1892."

"True. But George, that was thirty years ago. Styles change. People around here say, 'There goes the great Professor Carver. He looks like a ragamuffin.' "

"Then let the people in Washington say the same thing!"

"You are hopeless. Do you know what that last reporter said about you in the newspaper?"

"What?"

"He said you were a shabby, toothless old man."

"Do say. Why he just made the whole thing up. If he'd only asked me, I would have shown him I'm not toothless at all, for in my pocket I had

GUESS	1. my hands."
	2. my feet."
	3. my teeth."

"I had my teeth in my pocket the whole time."

115

Booker T. Washington held up his hands. "I give up. The Lord takes care of fools and idiots for sure." He patted George on the back. "God bless you, George Carver!"

George arrived at the steps of the House of Representatives. Someone snickered. "His clothes look like they were cut by an axe before the Civil War."

Friends were watching for him. They hurried him to the chambers of Congress where the meeting was being held.

"Here, let us carry those heavy boxes," his friends urged. Then together they sat down and

GUESS	1. waited. 2. sang. 3. laughed.

They waited for a couple of hours. Some people left for food. "I'm glad I brought this bologna sandwich to eat on the train," George said, eating happily. His friends said they weren't hungry.

Late in the afternoon, the chairman rapped for order and said, "Professor Carver, it is late. Most congressmen have already made up their minds, anyway, so we are cutting your time to ten minutes."

George stumbled up the aisle to the platform with his heavy wooden boxes. He opened them and started taking out bottles and small cartons.

Questions poured out from the congressmen. George answered quietly, still taking out his display.

When he was ready, he said, "You have already taken three of my minutes. I presume you will give them back."

The men stopped talking. When it was quiet, Goerge picked up a piece of candy from his exhibit.

"This is chocolate covered candy," he said. "You can't taste it, so I'll taste it for you."

When the laughter stopped, he held up a bottle and began to talk. The men

GUESS	1. were restless. 2. went home.

3. listened to every word.

Carver showed his stains for leather and for wood. He asked the men to try his fruit punch and his instant coffee with cream, all made from peanuts.

At the end of ten minutes, he started to pack up his things. Everyone cried,

GUESS

1. "Hurry up, old man!"
2. "Don't stop!"
3. "We are tired."

"Don't stop!" everyone cried. "Tell us more!"

George showed his buttermilk and evaporated milk. After an hour of demonstrating, he said, "The boll weevil has put the South in the poorhouse. But if companies buy peanuts to make these products I've shown you, the South can rise again."

"How many products have you found?" someone asked.

"I found one hundred eighteen uses for the sweet potato and over three hundred uses for the peanut."

The men rose to their feet and applauded.

After the speech, they surrounded him.

"How do you know what to look for?"

"God has said that every herb and plant that He created can be useful to mankind, if we will only put our hand in His and let Him help us."

"Where were you educated?"

"Iowa State University. I have a Master's Degree in Agriculture."

"Are you married?"

George answered,

GUESS

1. "I never had time."
2. "I didn't want my work interrupted."
3. "I never found anyone."

George said, "A wife would only interrupt my work."

117

"You are certainly wonderful."

"No, sir, I'm not. If I were not here, God would find someone else to do His work. That He chose me is no credit to me."

"Perhaps not," a Congressman said, "It was truly God's wisdom."

As George rode home from Washington, he looked out the train windows. Approaching Alabama, he saw farms with painted houses, vegetable gardens, chicken yards, hog pens. The soil looked healthy. Gone were the washed-out gullies. He smiled and spoke to the man sitting beside him.

"You a farmer?"

"Yes, sir," the black man answered. "One of them smarty younguns, Tom Campbell from the Tuskegee School, done talked me into saving five cents every working day. In a year, I had fifteen dollars and fifty cents, enough to buy three acres of land, with fifty cents left over."

"Yes. Tell me more."

"Course the land were done wore out, but I did what that whipper-snapper done told me, and it changed back like land should be. I raise tomatoes—and eat them, too."

"You didn't eat them before?"

"No, sir. I done heard they was poison." George let the man rest until he spoke up again. "We got chickens and a cow. We eats fruits, nuts, vegetables, butter, cheese, eggs, cured meat, and pre-serves."

"How about peanuts?"

"Where you been, man? Peanuts is our cash crop. They will give us our living, now they passed the Hawley-Smoot Bill yester-day."

"And you live well," George said.

"That we does. How did you know?"

George went back to Tuskegee Institute and to his laboratory a happy man.

"Now that you are seventy-five years old," Booker told him, "take it easy. Don't get up at four A.M. Rest a bit!"

"Why?" George looked at him in astonishment. "The dawn does not come twice to wake a man. That's when I talk to God and get my directions for the day."

He continued

1. getting up.

GUESS　　2. experimenting.

3. racing.

George kept on experimenting. He originated thirty different kinds of cattle feed and also special feeds to produce more bacon and ham.

Booker T. Washington insisted George have

GUESS

1. a new watch.

2. a new house.

3. an assistant.

His new assistant was Austin Curtis.

One day Curtis scolded George for walking to the dining hall without a coat on.

"It is amazing, you know," said George, "that I have managed to survive all these years without you."

"Only by the sheerest luck," Curtis answered.

"You are turning into a pest, young man," George replied, in good humor.

"That must be, sir. Everyone says I am getting more like Professor Carver every day."

In 1939 George had a visitor. It was

GUESS

1. Franklin D. Roosevelt.

2. Henry Wallace.

3. Moses Carver.

One day the President of the United States, Franklin Roosevelt, came to visit George.

"Pardon me, sir, but let me talk first to your Vice-President, Henry Wallace. Henry, is it really you?" George asked.

"Yes, sir. Remember how I tagged after you in the greenhouse?"

"Could never forget! You were the closest to a son I ever had.

119

"Welcome, President Roosevelt."

Made me proud, too, Mr. Vice-President!"

"Not as proud as I am of you!"

George Carver died on January 5, 1943, sitting in his chair. At his funeral his favorite hymn was sung—"Out in the Fields with God."

Later, President Harry S. Truman introduced a bill to establish a monument in honor of George Washington Carver. On it are these words: "He could have added fortune to fame, but caring for neither, he found happiness and honor in being helpful to the world."

But George Washington Carver said of himself, "It is not we little men who do the work, but the Creator working through us. . . . The secret lies in the promises of God. They are real, but so few people believe them."

Moody Press, a ministry of the Moody Bible Institute, is designed for education, evangelization, and edification. If we may assist you in knowing more about Christ and the Christian life, please write us without obligation: Moody Press, c/o MLM, Chicago, Illinois 60610.